Losing Faith in the BBC

at a crucial time for
Religious Broadcasting
in Great Britain

Nigel Holmes is a member of the General Synod of
the Church of England, of its Board of Mission and
of the Churches' Advisory Council for Local Broadcasting. He is Chairman of the Editorial Committee
of the Central Readers' Council, Chairman of the
Carlisle Diocesan Synod and a Reader in the
Diocese. He was a member of the Church of England
Committee for Communications and a BBC Radio
Producer for almost 30 years, during which time he
won Sandford St. Martin and Andrew Cross Awards
for religious broadcasting.

Losing Faith in the BBC

at a crucial time for
Religious Broadcasting
in Great Britain

Nigel Holmes

paternoster
press

First Published 2000 by Paternoster Press

06 05 04 03 02 01 00   7 6 5 4 3 2 1

Paternoster Press is an imprint of Paternoster Publishing,
PO Box 300, Carlisle, Cumbria, CA3 0QS, UK
and Paternoster Publishing USA
Box 1047, Waynesboro, GA 30830-2047
www.paternoster-publishing.com

British Library Cataloguing in Publication Data

A catalogue record for this book is available
from the British Library
1-84227-039-7

Typeset by WestKey, Falmouth, Cornwall
Cover design by Diane Bainbridge
Printed in Great Britain

Dedicated to my wife,
Susan, who loathes publicity.

Contents

Look at What You Can No Longer Hear

Hours devoted to religious television have been reduced whilst overall output has increased greatly.

Serious Sunday evening television programmes have fallen from 48 a year in 1987/88 to 20 a year in 1999/2000.

Sunday evening television programmes have been scheduled ever later, sometimes starting at 11.45 p.m.

Radio 4 programmes have been scheduled for early in the morning or very late at night.

Sunday is shorter – 45 minutes from 7.10 a.m. instead of 55 minutes from 7.40 a.m.

Sunday Worship is shorter – 38 minutes from 8.07 a.m. instead of 45 minutes from 9.30 a.m.

No devotional BBC radio or television programmes on Sunday mornings after 8.45 a.m.

Something Understood was reduced by 20 minutes, finishing earlier at 6.35 a.m.

Prayer for the Day was switched to 5.45 a.m. (from 6.25 a.m.) and shortened from five to two minutes; from

April 2000 to 5.43 a.m. with no advance notice (although the *Radio Times* still listed the start time at 5.45 a.m.).

The length of *Thought for the Day* has been reduced to two minutes and forty-five seconds.

Radio 4 has cut *Seeds of Faith, Soundings, The Week in Synod* and *The Royal Maundy*.

The *Daily Service* has been confined to long-wave Radio 4 only.

First the Saturday *Daily Service* was removed from the morning schedule in the 1980s, then *Ten to Ten* disappeared from Saturday evenings in 1998 ending 70 years of daily worship.

Songs of Praise has been moved to 5.25 p.m., an hour earlier than the traditional placing and is no longer in peak time.

The Moral Maze has been moved from peak time to off-peak – 9.03 a.m. to 8.03 p.m.

Since 1993/94 there have been no religious programmes on Radio 1 (according to the BBC's own figures).

When Radio 5 became Radio 5 Live, religious programmes disappeared from the schedules.

Serious coverage of religion for younger listeners and viewers has not been evident for many years.

Fewer major ambitious series relating to religion, with accompanying books, on radio or television recently.

There is no longer a high profile national Religious Affairs Correspondent.

At Easter 2000, Radio 4 played the Easter Hymn at the start of transmission, not at 7 a.m. and 8 a.m.

Introduction

England's oldest national institution challenges its youngest

> It is rare for great British institutions to fall out ... Although it is late in the day for the Church to take on the Corporation, the battle is not yet lost, as many would like to be told how to pray and enjoy being shown how to boil an egg ... The potential for a new Delia of the God slot ought to make even Greg Dyke's BBC relish synergy with the Synod.
>
> (*The Daily Telegraph*, 15 February 2000)

From modest aspirations early in 1999, the national debate over the future of religious broadcasting culminated in a resounding vote of regret over the reduction and rescheduling of religious programmes (General Synod, Spring 2000 Group of Sessions). Few Private Members' Motions end with a vote of 370 to nil. In the churches, few apart from bishops and other denominational leaders prompt such comprehensive press coverage or receive letters in large numbers from people throughout the country.

In this case, the timing appears to have been just right to strike a chord with so many who felt that all was far from well in British religious broadcasting but had no yardstick by which to measure change. What I did, at the behest of the Churches' Advisory Council for Local Broadcasting on which I am a Church of England representative, was to follow a line of research based initially on an intuitive hunch – the increasing marginalization of transmission times for religious programmes.

So I drafted a 24-page report, *Losing Faith in the BBC* – no colour, no frills, but packed with facts and figures and the views of informed observers – which was distributed to General Synod members in November 1999. As a result, a record 226 signed in support of my Private Member's Motion, thus securing a debate during the following Group of Sessions. This is an expanded version of that report.

The key fact to emerge was that whilst the total output of BBC 1 and BBC 2 combined had increased by a half within the span of ten years, the hours devoted to religious broadcasting had fallen by one-third. That highlighted the scale of the decline which could not be ignored; similarly, the network religious radio figure was down by an unprecedented 15 per cent between 1997/98 and 1998/99. An organization like the BBC is adept at rebutting external pressure; however, in this case it could not dispute the figures for they were the Corporation's own, published in their Annual Reports.

The publicity that resulted was quite staggering. *The Sunday Telegraph* was the first to run a sizeable article in November, the media section of *The Independent* used the report in the week before Christmas and *The Times* looked ahead to the forthcoming debate in an issue during January. Then early in February, when the agenda for the Synod was announced, all the broadsheets, as well as *The Mail, The Express,* the London *Evening Standard* and, perhaps most surprising, the front page of *The Scotsman,* detailed the contents of the report. Then the feature pages began to take an interest with *The Guardian* requesting a letter exchange with the Head of BBC Religious Broadcasting. *The Daily Telegraph* and *The Times* radio critics joined in. *The Sunday Times* (20 February 2000) ran an article under the headline: 'BBC to aim religious broadcasting at the feng shui tendency' accompanied by a cartoon. The Head of Religious Broadcasting was pictured on his knees with the bubble containing the words: 'To whomsoever it may concern ...' (see Appendix A for a digest of the press coverage).

As the debate grew closer there were invitations to appear on the Radio 4 arts and religious programmes and on BBC breakfast television and GMTV. Joan Bakewell's public resignation from *Heart of the Matter* in February 2000 because of its increasingly late transmission time, year-on-year budget cuts and general BBC 'neglect' of religious broadcasting fuelled the coverage.

The debate itself on Leap Year Day 2000, showed Synod at its best. A deep pool of professional knowledge of broadcasting and media politics was tapped, yet more was said in sorrow than in anger. Whilst the serious nature of the concerns was shared by all, the tone was one of encouraging rather than chastising the BBC. The amended motion, passed by 370 votes to nil, said that this Synod:

a) express its gratitude to broadcasters who have, over the years, accurately reflected and vastly enriched the spiritual life of the nation with coherent, intelligent, entertaining and engaging religious broadcasts;

b) regret the reduction and rescheduling of certain religious broadcasts by the BBC and call on the Corporation, in the context of their public service commitments and statutory responsibilities to a changing society, to maintain and develop high quality religious programmes, including worship especially for the housebound, for present and future analogue and digital channels which are made to high production values, designed for a general audience, including young people, and carried at peak listening and viewing times;

c) call on the Churches to support and engage with those involved in broadcasting in creative and imaginative ways, helping our culture to explore faith not as an additional element to an otherwise secular world but as a part of it;

d) ask the Archbishops' Council to develop, in co-operation with other Churches and interested parties, a mechanism for monitoring and reporting on the provision and quality of religious output by the BBC and the commercial sector.

(General Synod of the Church of England,
29 February 2000)

The motion had been amended by the Bishop of Wakefield, by Peter Mullins on behalf of the Lincoln Diocesan Synod, and by David Webster from Rochester, who had himself once interviewed Lord Reith. I am sure the founder of the BBC would have applauded the result in the context of the decline in the concern of the Corporation for religious broadcasting (see Appendix B for a summary of the debate).

Those who have the power and privilege now, the Governors and the new Director-General, cannot but take this show of solidarity seriously, particularly as after the Synod debate the ecumenical body, Council of Churches for Britain and Ireland, said it wanted to take the issue forward with support from across the denominations. Concessions had been offered prior to the debate. *Everyman* was to be screened up to an hour earlier and no later than 10.40 p.m. Just two days before the debate it was announced that the repeat of *Songs of Praise*, dropped five years previously, was to be restored to the schedule. While those moves were welcome, they did not involve fresh resources or programme creativity.

The aim now must be to recoup as much as possible of the £250,000 taken from the budget of BBC Religious Broadcasting and to encourage other areas of production, such as drama, to reflect the spiritual dimension. (As early as 1953, Colin Beale, the first full-time Religious Broadcasting Organizer in BBC Television, advocated the adventurous use of drama and film to exploit to the full the visual nature of the medium.) The BBC's own surveys prove that good religious broadcasting can win sizeable audiences, as ITV found over Christmas 1999 with *Bethlehem Year Zero*. ITV and Channel 4 have been leading in fresh ideas in recent years, even bringing serious spiritual content to a youth audience in an imaginative way.

The Synod debate also proved the worth of BBC Local Radio. Speaker after speaker felt that this highly valued BBC service, second only to BBC 1 television, had achieved so much on so little and was being cut even further. At the time of the debate, religious radio in BBC Wales was threatened with 40 per cent cuts which would have removed half the staff and seen the end of broadcast worship. There the Archbishop of Wales, Rowan Williams and the Welsh ecumenical organization galvanized the opposition, which prompted petitions and at least 700 letters from individuals. A fortnight after the Synod debate, the Controller of BBC Wales decided not to make any changes to the religious output for at least a year.

The Bishop of Wakefield told the Synod that he hoped that the Archbishops' Council would establish a system of monitoring the network religious output both of the BBC and commercial broadcasters, so that never again could so much be lost. The Archbishop of York, who is also Chairman of the Central Religious Advisory Committee (CRAC) of the BBC and the Independent Television Commission, expressed the hope that in time CRAC would perhaps be reconstituted in such a way that it could exert more influence.

Other faiths have representatives who are members of CRAC, and there is common dissatisfaction across the faiths over religious coverage. This is not an issue that sets Christians apart. The minorities recognize that there are at least ten times as many active Christians as active Muslims and that active members of all non-Christian faiths total less than five per cent of the United Kingdom population.

> The BBC is one of the twentieth century's great inventions, enjoyed by its audiences at home and admired around the globe for the quality, the originality, the wit and intelligence of its programmes.
>
> (BBC Chairman and Director-General,
> Introduction to *The BBC Beyond 2000*,
> December 1998)

> I am determined to ensure that religious broadcasting in England is robust and serves the Gospel and the people.
>
> (The Archbishop of York,
> Chairman of CRAC,
> July 1999)

With a new Director-General and a new Controller of Radio 4, now is a better time than in the recent past to persuade the BBC to write 'public service broadcasting' in rather larger letters. The Corporation must, apart from anything else, demonstrate to the many millions who have an active faith, and the many more who are interested in the spiritual dimension of human life, that it deserves the licence fee, which has been set by the Government above the level of inflation in order to fund digital developments. The digital channels, which have appeared so far, have yet to make that case convincingly.

Religious programmes take their chances in the mainstream against whatever the opposition cares to put up. And the size of the budgets reflects the challenge. Religious producers now handle with practised ease huge drama budgets and resources and mount high-cost documentaries on both radio and television.

(BBC Annual Report 1987)

The *BBC Annual Report 1987* covered the programme year 1985/86, which was capped for the Religious Broadcasting Department with the BAFTA award for the best single drama of the year, *Shadowlands*, about the brief and tragic marriage of C.S. Lewis to Joy Davidman. It was a very different broadcasting environment in which Dr Lewis himself first contributed to BBC radio before the Second World War. The story of religious broadcasting development is one of growth in quantity and of audience appreciation of quality up to and including the 1980s. As one year succeeds another, it is difficult to place change in context and perspective. Our memories are both selective and subjective, which is why the BBC's own facts, figures and statements, drawn from many documents published in recent years, form the backbone of this analysis.

The BBC Beyond 2000, the most recent 22-page strategy document, makes no mention of religion. The closest it comes, is to say: 'In this new world, the BBC's public purposes are all important. In a new age some of these are unchanged ... to provide something of particular value to all UK licence payers, exposing audiences to new ideas, scientific discovery, to great art, music and writing, to the spiritual and uplifting.' In the full 86-page version of this document, the word 'religion' is mentioned twice. On page 14 under the chapter heading 'The Changing World', we are told: 'Distinctions can be made based on differences in age, income, educational opportunity, the urban/

rural divide, religion, ethnic background or the differences between the regions and nations of the United Kingdom.' On page 26 within the chapter 'Choice, Distinctiveness and Creativity', we read: 'BBC Radio has a particular role in exploring and explaining the key issues in modern society – whether in science, politics, the arts, history, philosophy or religion.'

There is precious little about BBC Religious Broadcasting beyond 2000, but perhaps the minimal mention says more than many words. The publication of that booklet coincided with a Religious Broadcasting Department meeting in Manchester to announce a new *Strategy for the Future*, at which it was said that eleven producer posts would have to be shed because of a £250,000 drop in funding for the Department. Just over six months later the Department issued its own strategy paper, *BBC Religion – Into the Third Millennium*. This paper proved to be an embarrassment to the BBC centrally, which itself took charge of revising the strategy of BBC Religious Broadcasting just nine months after *BBC Religion – Into the Third Millennium* had been published.

Whilst the hours of BBC transmission have greatly increased over the past decade, both in network radio and television, the representation of religion in general and Christianity in particular has diminished. What remains has been pushed to the margins of the schedules, to times when it is ever more difficult to attract a sizeable audience.

This report is an attempt to chronicle the achievements of the BBC, which have been substantial, and to analyse those changes of recent years, including many which may be thought detrimental, as fairly as possible.

If media influence is only one-half of what is commonly supposed, it still requires believers to take it seriously ... As Christians we have an interest in sustaining the conviction that the full potential of television and radio should be employed to enrich the human mind, heart and spirit … If broadcasting trivialises its content, it trivialises itself.

> (the late Archbishop Robert Runcie,
> Church of England General Synod Debate,
> February 1989)

You might like to express your views, for taking the trouble to praise or criticize does make a difference. The main addresses are:

BBC Governors, Broadcasting House, London, W1A 1AA
e-mail: info@bbc.co.uk
web: www.bbc.co.uk

The Broadcasting Policy Branch, The Department for Culture, Media and Sport, 2–4 Cockspur Street, London SW1Y 5DH
e-mail: name.name@culture.gov.uk
web: www.culture.gov.uk

The Independent Television Commission, 33 Foley Street, London W1P 7LB
e-mail: publicaffairs@itc.org.uk
web: www.itc.org.uk

The Radio Authority, Holbrook House, 14 Great Queen Street, London WC2 5DG
e-mail: info@radioauthority.org.uk
web: www.radioauthority.org.uk

> Nigel Holmes
> Great Corby, Carlisle
> e-mail: nigel@gt-corby.demon.co.uk
> *Midsummer 2000*

Democratic Deficit – Spiritual Deficit

BBC Television output up by a half – religious output down by a third

> The Christian religion is part of our culture. Religious broad-
> casting is not for a minority, especially when we begin to add
> the other faith communities. It is about broadcasting to the
> whole person, in the mainstream.
>
> (The Right Reverend James Jones, Bishop of Liverpool)

For those outside the BBC, it is hard to obtain detailed
audience figures, but we do know that the earlier placing
of *Sunday* on Radio 4 initially resulted in a 25 per cent loss
of peak audience from 1.6 million before the changes. It
seems certain that moving *The Moral Maze* from 9 a.m. to
8 p.m. lost at least two-thirds.

We know that the audience for *Yesterday in Parliament*
fell by 73 per cent when transferred to long wave only in
1998. The same fate befell the *Daily Service* some years
before. But parliamentarians have put up a fight and the
BBC has listened to their case. Within the span of nine
weeks early in 1999, concern over the future of public
service broadcasting prompted no less than three debates
in the House of Lords and one, concentrating on parliamentary broadcasting, in the House of Commons. The
first in the Lords was requested by Lord Bragg; that in the

Commons by another former BBC producer, Denis MacShane, MP, who once worked for BBC Radio London. The parliamentary and religious parallels are marked. The audience figures resulting from the changes to parliamentary coverage in 1998 were stark. Overall reach was down 26 per cent. *Yesterday in Parliament* was only attracting 830,000 against 3.13 million before the change to long wave only in April 1998, and *The Week in Westminster* just a third of its previous following; in other words down 65 per cent.

Mr MacShane quoted from a contrite letter from the Chairman of the BBC, Sir Christopher Bland:

> The BBC should be, and I believe is, big enough to put things right when mistakes have been made. Two things are clear. The loss of listeners is much greater than we had expected, and that whatever the cause of the loss, there is an unacceptable "democratic deficit" which the BBC, with its special public service responsibilities, needs to address. The BBC must give appropriate prominence to coverage of parliamentary proceedings.
>
> (*Hansard*, 14 April 1999)

Twelve months earlier, the BBC had maintained that 'what we have attempted to do with the new [Radio 4] schedule is to enhance our coverage and place it [Parliamentary coverage] where its audience will appreciate it most. Radio 4 listeners are particularly receptive to this sort of programming' (BBC staff newspaper, *Ariel*, 1998). A year later, the BBC told parliamentarians that it was open to change and wished to identify the best way of reconciling the competing interests of different audiences.

Paul Tyler, MP, speaking in the debate, said that the BBC was treating the proceedings of the House of Commons as an esoteric, odd and peculiar hobby of a very few people.

Much the same attitude would appear to apply to religious broadcasting. Denis MacShane commented: 'I welcome a sinner who is prepared to convert and I hope that the Chairman will put his words into practice.' He went on to call on backbenchers to 'Dare to be a Daniel, dare to stand alone, dare to have a purpose firm and dare to make it known' (*Hansard*, 14 April 1999). He said that strong backbench voices were necessary.

As a result of this political pressure, the BBC Governors decided that from the start of the new parliamentary year, in October 1999, *The Week in Westminster* would be restored to its former Saturday morning slot on both FM and long wave, and *Today in Parliament* would return five nights a week to both frequencies. In addition, there is a daily *Yesterday in Parliament* briefing at 6.45 a.m. on both frequencies within the *Today* programme. Furthermore, a greater amount of trailing is guaranteed for parliamentary programmes. The Governors had concluded 'that such a loss in audience reach did not represent "appropriate prominence" for parliamentary broadcasting. It is clear to us that we need to take action. We believe this package offers a reasonable way forward which will restore audience reach to parliamentary broadcasting on Radio 4, while ensuring that the network can fulfil its other public service obligations and respond to audience preferences' (*Ariel*, 1999). They also believed that there should be improved marketing of the BBC's parliamentary coverage on all media and that the BBC's responsibilities to political debate should be continuously reviewed. The Chairman of the BBC admitted that the loss of audience to parliamentary programmes had created 'an unacceptable democratic deficit'. Should he not be prevailed upon to acknowledge an ever deeper spiritual deficit within the output of the BBC?

There is a close parallel between church and state.

Parliamentary leaders trusted the BBC to fulfil its public service obligations, just as church leaders have for more than three-quarters of a century. MPs have the great advantage that they ultimately control the licence fee, as was pointed out in that debate. At the very time the debate was taking place, 14 April 1999, the BBC was floating the idea of an extra £39 licence fee for digital, on top of the £101 colour television licence fee. The Committee chaired by Gavyn Davies, in August 1999, proposed much less – £24 a year from April 2000, falling to £12 by 2006 – as it was said not to have been convinced by the BBC's request for an extra £650 million from the digital supplement.

In the event the BBC was granted one-third of what it had sought. The universal fee rose by £3 to £104 in April 2000 and will rise by 1.5 per cent above inflation for the next seven years giving the BBC another £200 million a year. (This is, incidentally, sufficient to cover the employment costs of all the clergy of the Church of England.) The Culture Secretary, Chris Smith, also announced that there would be reviews of all the existing BBC digital channels and said that he did not expect the licence fee to fund 'strands of the market, such as dedicated film and sport channels, to which the distinctive role of public service broadcasting has little extra to offer' (*The Guardian*, 4 February 2000).

BBC 1 has been struggling, holding just 28.2 per cent of all viewing compared to ITV's 39 per cent. Mr Smith welcomed the BBC's intention to 're-establish BBC 1 as the Corporation's flagship and its commitment to education, in particular learning support for schools and for life-long learning' (*The Guardian*, 22 February 2000). He accompanied the licence fee rise with a requirement on the Corporation to raise an additional £1.1 billion over seven years. The BBC had indicated that £600 million could be raised from savings and commercial ventures. The Corporation will face a tough challenge to strengthen its mainstream channels at the same time as developing its new digital outlets and BBC Online.

The output figures, particularly over the past ten years, speak for themselves. In 1987/88 BBC 1 and BBC 2 broadcast 11,559 hours of which 177 were described by the BBC as religious (1.5 per cent). The comparable totals for 1996/97 are 15,212 hours, of which 122 were religious (0.8 per cent), and for 1997/98, 15,876 with even fewer religious hours, 112. This last represents one hour in 140 hours or, alternatively, only 0.7 per cent of BBC network television is now defined by the BBC as religious. In 1998/99 the hours increased by 10 to 122 but fell back to 117 in 1999/2000, though the proportion of output remained the same at 0.7 per cent. As we will see later, the figures included new programmes, which the BBC classifies as 'religious' but which offer, in the main, trivial treatment of issues which deserve higher production values befitting subjects of a spiritual nature. Public service imperatives seem conveniently to be forgotten in the search to maximize audiences at the same time as minimizing cost.

According to the BBC's own figures published in Handbooks and Annual Reports, the most dramatic decline has occurred on BBC 2. In 1995/96 the channel carried 42 hours of religious programmes, in 1996/97 16 hours and in 1997/98 a mere seven, one of which was a repeat. So in two years BBC 2 removed five-sixths of its religious programmes, surely an unprecedented rate of loss of any category of output in the history of the Corporation. The figures for BBC 1 have remained stable in the past few years: 110 hours in 1995/96, 106 in 1996/97, 105 in 1997/98, 112 in 1998/99 and 105 in 1999/2000. However, in 1985/86 the comparable output was 156 hours. Furthermore, the placing of religious programmes has been increasingly during off-peak hours. The *BBC Annual Report 1998/99* acknowledged for the first time that there were no longer any religious television programmes broadcast regularly in peak time. This is a consequence of the ever earlier placing of *Songs of Praise* which has now usually ended by 6 p.m. (see Appendix E for BBC United Kingdom religious output figures, 1950–2000).

> Whilst the overall output of BBC 1 and BBC 2 increased by a half over the ten years to 1997/98, religious broadcasting on those BBC channels fell by more than one-third.

Across the two television channels in 1997, sport boasted fourteen times the number of hours devoted to religious programmes, yet far more people attend a place of worship on a given Sunday than visit a sporting event on a Saturday. In passing, it is interesting to compare snooker coverage on BBC television during Holy Week 2000. I checked the *Radio Times* to find 41 hours 25 minutes devoted to snooker and only 7 hours 50 minutes to religious programmes. What was more, 10 hours 30 minutes of the snooker was in peak time compared to only 1 hour 5 minutes of the religious programmes. The film, *The Bible*, which accounted for 3 hours, more than a third of the week's total religious output, began as early as 6.30 a.m. on Holy Saturday morning. *Easter Tales*, the Holy Week drama series was broadcast so late the distinguished producer and cast complained publicly (see Appendix A for the extract from *The Sunday Telegraph*, 16 April 2000).

The percentage of religious programmes within network radio output in 1998/99 was one per cent. This is precisely half the time allocated to programme introductions and trails. The religious hours fell by 15.25 per cent in a single year (1997/98 to 1998/99), whilst the time devoted to overall programme presentation and promotion increased by a quarter within that one year. Sixty years earlier, in 1936, the airtime accorded to religion was 6.24 per cent. Of BBC terrestrial television analogue output, in 1962/63 4.1 per cent was religious; on the latest published figures it is one-sixth of that.

The BBC does not contest any of these figures, which have been drawn from its own publications. However, it does speak of its 'sloppy accounting', by which it means that only those programmes originating in the Religious Broadcasting Department are classified as religious. However, that still allows a fair comparison of like with like over the years and the additional programme hours, which we are told go unrecorded, are relatively few. The bulletin of the Department, issued in April 2000, pointed to about five hours of television that fell into this category but they were 1999/2000 figures, which had not then been published or quoted.

The BBC did put more effort into Christmas 1999 and New Year 2000 religious representation than for many years. On the first Sunday of 2000, BBC 2 covered the national church services and BBC 1 carried a live *Songs of Praise* from the new stadium in Cardiff that was packed with 66,000 people.

Such coverage can easily be justified when there are 36.5 million active or nominal Christians in the UK. The other faith dimension is minuscule by comparison. According to the Bishop of Bristol: 'Every Sunday in this land six million people attend places of worship.' At that time the minimal coverage given to Christianity the previous Christmas was fresh in the minds of many. The Bishop went on to say: 'Measured against religious programming in earlier years, there has been a decline. Measured against the substantial increase in BBC output, the decline has been considerable. Marginalization can produce a vicious circle in which the audiences may fall as a result of unfavourable scheduling, the commitment and available skill-base of programme makers and broadcasters is eroded, and so the marginalisation accelerates' (House of Lords, March 1999). He also observed that the shorter version of *The BBC Beyond 2000* 'makes no mention of religion whatsoever'.

In the later Lords debate, the Bishop of Wakefield said:

> The manner in which, for the most part, public service broad-casters now treat religion causes me dismay – a dismay I know to be shared in your Lordships' House beyond these [the Bishops'] Benches ... Ever more disturbing is the incontrovertible fact that on the mainstream channels, religious programmes have, for the most part, been pushed from prime time to the margins of the broadcast schedules, making them potentially less accessible to audiences, thereby diminishing the status of religious programmes and endangering their quality. That is such a tragedy because some of the best examples of public service broadcasting have been religious programmes. Without them the ability of public service broadcasting to maintain its standards of creative and imaginative programmes which inspire and enlighten and to provide a range of broadcasts, which not only reflect but also challenge, will be seriously undermined.
>
> (*Hansard*, 5 May 1999)

What is particularly noteworthy is the fact that, despite the relative paucity of religious output compared to, say, news or drama, many people do choose to encounter religious programming. It is unlikely, judging from this analysis, that very many viewers are loyal or watch particularly frequently, rather that a large number of people dip in on a relatively occasional basis. This is clear evidence that religious output, despite some criticism about its style and approach, is by no means the anathema for viewers that is supposed from the purely commercial viewpoint of some broadcasters.

(*Godwatching*, IBA, 1988)

In their 1992 survey, Hollis and Brent, found that 88 per cent of the population wanted the same or more religious broadcasting on television, only 12 per cent would have preferred less; 60 per cent of viewers agreed that it was not necessary to be religious to enjoy religious programmes and 17 per cent of those who say that they are not at all religious also say they sometimes watch religious programmes. In 1995, BBC Audience Research found that 'over 80 per cent want at least the present level of religious programmes on television, but since 29 per cent of the population claim to be non-religious, it appears that religious programmes appeal to many non-religious people. There is a significant demand for programmes about ethical and religious issues.' In the five years since that survey, BBC television religious output has fallen by 20 per cent.

The Head of BBC Local and Regional Programmes (South and West), Leo Devine, speaking in June 1999 at a conference organized by the Churches' Advisory Council for Local Broadcasting, quoted BBC research which had indicated that although only 20 per cent attend church regularly, a massive 78 per cent recognize Christianity as the 'backbone of their spirituality'. It had also shown that 'in some respects religion is more popular than sport'. At the same conference it was also mentioned that a Church of England initiative, the *Alpha* course, has attracted no fewer than 750,000 to serious sustained study of the essentials of the faith since 1992.

Three years before that, *A Matter of Respect*, a report from the Church of England Committee for Communications, stated: 'In view of the tendency of some senior broadcasters and other opinion-formers to imagine that religion belongs at the margins of human interest, it cannot be said too often that churchgoing is still the most popular, voluntary communal activity of the British people and that audiences for religious programmes reflect an even wider interest' (Church House Publishing, 1989). A decade later, the Executive Director of Christian Research, Peter Brierley, pointed out that if all those who attended church in 1998 had bought a ticket on each occasion, 200 million tickets would have been sold. 'The number beats all tickets sold by premiership and league soccer matches eight-fold,' he wrote (*Quadrant*, Christian Research, 2000). The 355,000 people who visited the National Gallery exhibition of Christian art, *Seeing Salvation*, in 2000 made it their most successful free exhibition ever, almost double the previous record figure. Record sales (21,000) of the exhibition catalogue ensured it reached fourth place in the non-fiction best-seller lists behind *The Highway Code* and ahead of *Who Wants to be a Millionaire?* To the BBC's credit, they gave the Gallery's director, Neil MacGregor, himself a Christian, the opportunity to present four programmes at peak times on Sunday evenings on BBC 2.

The digital future is proclaimed in every BBC booklet and brochure, yet no mention is made of religious broadcasting in that context. Clearly it ought to be represented in the schedules of the digital channels, BBC Choice and BBC Knowledge. It is not, apart from the series, *Seeing*

Salvation, which secured a repeat on BBC Knowledge. The BBC describes the latter as 'A new TV and Internet service that offers you the opportunity to get more out of your life and work. With a wide range of programming available, from how to get ahead in your career to computing, you can explore as much or as little as you want' (BBC leaflet, 1999). Digital radio services will also offer more airtime and, it is to be hoped, scope for fresh religious opportunities. But for some years to come, most listening and viewing will be to the long-established analogue services. The first fight must be to regain some of the extensive ground that has recently been lost.

2

ITV Takes the Lead

Telling tales about BBC Promises

It was felt that because these dramas are considered, thoughtful pieces, they suit the later evening slots when the audience has time to sit and enjoy them.

(The Reverend Ernie Rea, Head of BBC Religious
Broadcasting, April 2000)

In marked contrast to the BBC performance, the volume of religious broadcasting on ITV has hardly changed since the 1980s – at 2 hours 12 minutes per week in 1998/99 (five minutes less than in the 1980s) which exceeds the ITC decreed minimum of two hours. The ITV network component is one hour and 54 minutes, plus ten minutes from GMTV. The regional component varies from five minutes to 26 minutes between the English stations, and in excess of an hour on some of the Scottish stations, but these latter take a smaller amount of the English network offering. This then, ignoring additional coverage of major festivals, totals more than 115 hours a year on average, exceeding the combined figure for the two BBC channels in 1997/98 by three hours. Again, between April and October 1999, ITV network religious programmes exceeded those on both BBC 1 and BBC 2 by more than 20 per cent.

With the ITC requirement for Channel 4 to carry one hour of religious programmes a week, the two main commercial television channels exceed 150 hours a year, almost half as much again as the two BBC public service channels achieve in total. Channel 5 produces a further hour a week. Since 1998, Channel 4, a public corporation like the BBC, has also carried the brief from the ITC to 'look for distinctive work and enlarge the scope and reach' of religious output by including some of the programmes in peak time. Channel 4 carries about ten times the religious output of BBC 2, substantially exceeding the number of hours required by the ITC. However, ITV no longer has an obligation to broadcast religious programmes in peak time; with 85 per cent of its revenue generated between 7 p.m. and 10 p.m., there is great commercial pressure to maximize audiences.

The BBC released figures in February 2000, showing that largely as a result of *Songs of Praise*, which alone attracts some five million viewers a week, the lion's share of religious television viewing is held by the BBC: BBC 1 (69 per cent), BBC 2 (2 per cent), ITV (23 per cent), Channel 4 (4 per cent) and Channel 5 (2 per cent).

At Christmas 1999, on six successive evenings ITV recreated, in television news format, the events of 2000 years ago in *Bethlehem Year Zero*. These well-researched programmes astounded the schedulers by attracting a late viewing audience in excess of four million viewers. This success prompted ITV to carry a further eight short programmes using a similar format in Holy Week 2000, under the title *Dateline Jerusalem*. The presenter was Martyn Lewis who attempted, with David Jessel, to put the events of the crucifixion and resurrection of Christ in the social and political context of the time. This series reminded me of what claimed to be 'the first weekly television programme about Christianity' called *About*

Religion produced by ABC Television from 1955 to 1962. In March 1961, 'modern techniques of television news were employed' in *Good Friday News* which added 'something in immediacy and impact to our understanding of the Crucifixion story'. *About Religion* was intentionally produced for the uncommitted. Michael Redington won the award of the Guild of Television Producers and Directors for Factual Programmes with this series which 'aimed at making religion in the best sense of the word – news'. He said he sought 'to give its message the immediacy, the impact of something experienced here and now, first-hand, for the first time'.

In that same Holy Week in which ITV ran *Dateline Jerusalem*, BBC 1 broadcast six imaginative and thought-provoking monologues (each lasting 15 minutes) for a rather different audience called *Easter Tales*. However, the times of transmission varied from 10.45 p.m. to midnight. This prompted *The Sunday Telegraph* to carry a page lead with the title: 'BBC relegates its Easter story to the graveyard slot'.

> The creators of a new BBC drama series for Easter starring Helen Baxendale, Jonathan Price and Joss Acland, have accused executives of broadcasting it late at night because it deals with religion ... In addition to an all-star cast, the series has attracted some leading writers, including the veteran playwright Arnold Wesker ... BBC executives changed its name to make it more obviously religious and then scheduled the monologues for the 'graveyard slot' with most appearing just before midnight.
>
> The Bishop of Liverpool said that the BBC remained deaf to the vast audience who wanted good religious programmes in the mainstream of broadcasting. Norman Stone, who produced the series, said that it had suffered from 'an ancient knee-jerk reaction that religion must be put on

late because it won't attract an audience'. Mr Stone created the award-winning *Shadowlands* about C.S. Lewis. Ernie Rea, the Head of BBC Religious Broadcasting said: 'It was felt that because these dramas are considered, thoughtful pieces, they suit the later evening slots when the audience has time to sit and enjoy them'.

(*The Sunday Telegraph*, 16 April 2000)

It should be pointed out that the transmission times were, on average, four minutes earlier than for the Bishop of Liverpool's BBC 1 series for Holy Week 1999, *Word on the Street* (which itself had attracted criticism for its late hour), and 15 minutes earlier than ITV's Holy Week 2000 series, *Dateline Jerusalem*.

ITV has attracted Sir David Frost, son of a Methodist minister, as presenter of its major Christian series of ten one-hour programmes to be screened in 2001. Sir David said that they will reflect his 'interests and concerns'. The series will feature ten people as they follow the hugely successful *Alpha* course initiated by the Church of England parish in London, Holy Trinity, Brompton.

Under its remit, Channel 4 does not have to win audience share in every slot. But it does no harm to expose religion in an accessible timeslot.

(Sarah Thane, Director of Programmes, ITC)

We aim our religious programmes at people who are not interested in religion – after all, everyone has faith in something.

(Peter Grimsdale, Channel 4 Commissioning Editor)

We are beginning to see a real ability to attract the top film-makers and putting these [religious] programmes out in prime time is tremendously important.

(Janice Hadlow, Channel 4 Commissioning Editor)

In its early days, Channel 5 broadcast Terry Waite's series *From Jesus to Christ* in peak time. Channel 5 spends about £500,000 a year on religious series. 'We are trying to bring religion out of the ghetto' (Nick Wilson, Controller of Children's and Religious Programmes).

ITV has run several series of a staggeringly popular Sunday morning animation for primary age children called *The Story Keepers*. It was the idea of a Methodist minister, the Reverend Brian Brown, and each programme amazingly is seen by almost half of 4- to 9-year-olds in the UK. It attracted a 29 per cent share of all age viewers at the time of its transmission and 40 per cent of the whole UK population has seen at least one episode. The series has sold well around the world. The programmes followed the adventures of Christians living in Rome in the early days of the church. Each week, four children dodged Roman soldiers to meet members of the Christian underground. In these secret meetings the believers swapped eyewitness accounts of 'the great storyteller – the one called Jesus'. Their mission was to keep alive the stories told by and about Jesus. Viewers saw Jesus telling a parable and then the characters putting it into action. *The Story Keepers* is now available for purchase on video cassette.

BBC Education has also produced programmes on video for use in schools: *Images of Jesus in Art*, derived from the general series *Seeing Salvation*, *The Miracle Maker* and *The Test of Time*. An impressive 90 per cent of secondary schools' religious education departments use BBC resources compared to 20 per cent little more than five years ago. The same department makes 56 new programmes of 'collective worship' each year for primary schools which are available on audio cassette. Given the scale of the recent success of BBC Education, it is all the more surprising that the BBC Religious

Department is not doing more for this age group outside school hours.

Parables were the theme behind ITV's late Sunday evening offering during Lent 2000, for the 15–25 age group. *What's It All About?* gave young people the chance to seek answers from internationally respected figures of faith. On Sunday mornings, *The Jesus File*, also on ITV, has brought the ancient Bible lands and events alive.

Whilst BBC Television and Radio have both marginalized religious programmes, BBC Radio remains unchallenged both in quality and range of religious output, nationally and locally. Nationally, the standard of BBC radio worship is probably as high as it has ever been under the guidance of the Reverend Stephen Shipley. BBC Local Radio does now require its stations to carry two hours of religious output a week, which is usually a magazine programme – a mixture of current affairs and music heard early on Sunday mornings. Sadly, since the resources available to BBC Local Radio have been declining for many years, so the standard of that output is, in some places, not as high as it once was. Some station budgets were cut by seven per cent from April 1999 and a further four per cent from April 2000, in spite of the fact that BBC Local Radio is the BBC's second most valued service after BBC 1 television. Nonetheless, as a result of great dedication by staff, percentage audiences are often greater than those for Radio 2 and Radio 4 combined early on Sunday mornings. Each week, 1.2 million tune into BBC Local Radio religious programmes. Indeed, BBC Radio Merseyside won a Sony Gold Award in 1999 for live coverage of the enthronement of the Bishop of Liverpool. The overall reach of BBC radio produced in Scotland and Wales and English local radio has risen by half a million in 2000 to a record 10.7 million listeners.

The former Director of Regional Broadcasting, Mark Byford, was keen to ensure that BBC Local Radio adequately reflected religion in its schedules. The report, *BBC Local Radio – 2000*, in contrast to *The BBC Beyond 2000*, devoted four and a half pages to religious broadcasting under the heading: 'Religious Output … an Obligation and an Audience Winner'.

> Religious output is an important part of our public service 'contract' and we will re-enforce our strongly-rooted tradition of recognising the different religious communities across England … Religious broadcasting on Sunday mornings is a big audience winner, capturing the biggest share of breakfast listening to BBC Local Radio across the week, averaging 15 per cent … Only sport on a Saturday afternoon attracts a higher average share, and only during the football season. Britain is still a predominantly Christian society, with 70 per cent of the population of 'vague faith' … These unchurched parishioners still feel an attachment to their faith of origin and in particular, an affinity with their local church. A high percentage of the elderly are particularly interested in religion and church affairs and often have a keen appetite for church news and religious programming with a local base. This is an important part of the heartland audience for BBC Local Radio. Churches of all denominations are landmarks of community identity, even for non-churchgoers … The output will be strengthened by the specialist expertise of our Religious Affairs Correspondent who provides reports, interviews and background information.
>
> (*BBC Local Radio – 2000: A review for a new era*, BBC, 1998)

Just two weeks after the General Synod debate, in March 2000, the Controller of English Regions, Andy Griffee, spoke at a regional briefing for local radio religious producers in the North. He said there were four particular genres in which the regions were expected to invest – one of which was religion. The warmer attitude to religious broadcasting extends to Scotland where, some will recall, over eight years William Barclay showed how the medium of television and the role of the Scots preacher could combine effectively. He had no props or visual tricks in his presentation of sound scholarship linked to popular anecdote. He was an enthusiast for the subject, a quality the medium captures and magnifies.

Coverage of the General Assembly of the Church of Scotland in 2000 is a good example of a very different attitude between schedulers and those who resource programme-making in BBC Scotland and London. During this week BBC Radio Scotland carried four special hour-long programmes at 9 p.m. of extra religious output. There was more special coverage on BBC Television Scotland and at peak time. BBC 2 Scotland carried four half-hour programmes, starting at either 8.00 or 8.30 p.m.; a total of two hours of debates and analysis. On the Wednesday there was a further one hour ten minutes coverage of the *Church and Nation* debate. In 1999, one of the speakers in that debate was the Bishop of Guildford. It seems strange that the Church of England observer at the General Assembly of the Church of Scotland can attract live coverage denied him at the General Synod of the Church of England. That is reflected only briefly in news programmes. The last live coverage was for the debate on the ordination of women to the priesthood seven years ago.

In Wales, the BBC picture is markedly less attractive than in Scotland. Early in 2000, proposals were tabled which would have removed two of the three radio producers working under the Head of the Religious Department and cut the budget by 40 per cent. The nature of the programmes was to be changed and broadcast worship ended. With the support of the Archbishop of Wales, Rowan Williams, and the Welsh ecumenical body hundreds of people wrote in opposition. The changes will not now be implemented 'for at least a year'.

In the commercial sector, the picture would also suggest that religious broadcasting is more vigorous in Scotland and Wales. A survey of commercial local radio in 1999 found that of 223 stations only 52 provided regular religious programmes, totalling 90 hours a week, most of which was Gospel music and 'Thoughts'. (For the first 20 years of commercial local radio there was a statutory requirement for them to include religious programmes.) However, in Scotland and Wales, religious broadcasting on commercial radio is more prominent, reflected in the comparatively high number of Andrew Cross Awards won by Scottish producers over the years.

BBC network radio hours of religious broadcasting were virtually the same in 1998/99 (439 hours) as they were in 1988/89 (428 hours) and indeed as in 1978/79 (419 hours). However, in that time total network output has grown by more than half as much again, from 27,889 hours in 1978/79 to 42,837 in 1998/99, partly as a result of the introduction of Radio 5 and, later, Radio 5 Live. In spite of its 8,760 hours a year, Radio 5 Live has carried no specifically religious programmes since its inception in 1994. The last recorded religious output on Radio 1 was two hours broadcast in the year 1993/94 (figures from BBC Annual Reports). Anecdotal evidence would suggest that the BBC has overlooked Radio 1 programmes broadcast at festivals, Christmas and Easter.

The BBC Annual Report 1998/99 ignores religion, as did *The BBC Beyond 2000* six months earlier. What is the reason? The space afforded to religion in the BBC's Annual Reports has declined markedly. In 1996/97 religion received twelve lines; ten years earlier it had been

deemed to be worth 160 lines and twenty years earlier
more than 300! In the *Annual Report 1997/98*, religion
ceased to have its own separate heading. Radio received
the briefest of coverage. Under the Radio 4 entry it
records: 'Radio 4 celebrated the 75th anniversary of the
BBC and the 70th anniversary of the *Daily Service*, which is
the longest-running daily programme in broadcasting
and another indication of Radio 4's ongoing commitment
to public service broadcasting.' Within a week of that
report year ending, Saturday evening worship ceased, so
ending 'daily' worship on BBC radio. What it did not hint
at were the reservations of the Head of Religious Broadcasting about the implications of the changes to the Radio
4 schedules implemented in April 1998. He has since
regretted 'the fact that the audience for the *Sunday*
programme has come down' and would 'like to see
[*Sunday*] moved to a later, more acceptable slot' (letter to
listener, 20 January 2000).

Television appeared in that report under 'Factual
Programmes'.

Religious broadcasting, based in Manchester, continue to
broaden their output to involve a more culturally diverse
audience, as well as seeking to interest those with no
religious views in more general spiritual and moral issues.
The panel assessing religious programmes commended
Songs of Praise for its imaginative selection of venues and
themes, but urged the BBC to make more programmes
appealing to young people and to reflect multi-faith Britain.
The BBC is working to accomplish this.

(BBC Annual Report 1997/98)

That was the total description of religious broadcasting,
yet two full pages of the report were devoted to
educational broadcasting.

The miracle is that in recent years we have enriched and increased the volume of BBC services ... We have expanded educational programming ... and funded much, much more.

(John Birt, then Director-General, *The McTaggart Lecture*,
August 1996)

Accessible and ambitious religious programming is a key part of our strategy for the BBC.

(Alan Yentob, then Director, BBC Television, October 1999)

The BBC constantly reviews its religious broadcasting and we are committed to reflecting the rich development of religious belief in Britain today.

(Greg Dyke, Director-General, 2000)

In broadcasting, and the BBC particularly, the idea that you should stretch the imagination and inspire people has been almost completely diluted by the need to get ratings. I think to myself, what kind of culture are we creating?

(Rory Bremner, 1999)

In November 1996, the BBC issued *Promises to Licence Payers*, which stated:

Religious broadcasting will always have an important place in the BBC. We promise to:

- provide additional religious programmes that are attractive to younger audiences
- reflect regional and cultural variations in belief and worship
- meet the needs of people whose faith is undefined with programmes which explore belief, meaning, purpose and value
- achieve an appropriate balance between the faiths
- broadcast programmes of religious worship, music and comment *at prominent places in the television and radio schedules* [my emphasis]

- reflect the religious life of local communities in our regional programmes, through informed and authoritative journalism and programming.

For Radio 2, the 'promise' was specific: 'To reflect a breadth of different faiths and beliefs, with daily editions of *Pause for Thought*, a weekly act of worship, *Sunday Half-Hour*, and a weekly programme featuring music and interviews on a religious theme, *Good Morning Sunday*' (*Promises to Licence Payers*, BBC, November 1996).

> The BBC should place particular priority on religious, moral and ethical programming which maintains *a prominent place in the radio and television schedules for programmes of religious worship, music and journalism* [my emphasis] ... and [explores] the major moral and ethical issues of our time ... BBC 1 should ... ensure that religious programmes retain a prominent place in the schedule. BBC 2 should ... ensure that programmes for special interest groups (whether of religious, ethnic or community interest) are offered when these groups are available to watch. [No coverage on BBC 1 between 6 p.m. and 11.30 p.m. – only 10 hours a year on BBC 2!] Radio should ... assign priority to those networks and services which are truly distinctive and unlikely ever to be matched in the commercial market place. [Out of earshot by 8.45!]
>
> *(Extending Choice – The BBC's role in the new broadcasting age, 1992)*

> The Governors attach great importance to the BBC's long-standing commitment to religious broadcasting. We are encouraged to see progress in religious programmes for the younger audience on BBC 1 and a growing number of commissions for Radio 1.
>
> *(BBC Annual Report 1995/96)*

The BBC Annual Reports state that there has been no religious output on Radio 1 since 1993/94 and none on Radio 5 Live since its inception in 1994, even though anecdotal evidence would suggest there have been occasional religious programmes and festivals, and, of course, news coverage. The Programme Strategy Review concluded that the BBC should develop a policy for each network for worship, religious culture and tradition which recognizes festivals and days of major religious significance. Yet in 1999, Religious Broadcasting in Manchester regarded neither Radio 1 nor 5 Live as 'markets where we will sell our output'. The Head of Department has said, in spite of this, that he is 'disappointed that Radio 1 no longer makes the rock documentaries that used to win Sony Awards' and recognizes that the BBC is failing to reach younger audiences with religion. He said he was glad a debate was underway.

3

Graveyard Spaces Reserved for Churches

Out of sight – out of mind

> The key point is that the great questions about life and death and the forces of good, evil, charity and faith never change. They are intrinsically interesting. Hardly ghetto subjects. They deserve greater attention.
>
> (Maggie Brown, *The Guardian*, 1999)

It is not only the number of hours of religious programmes broadcast, but the times at which they are scheduled and the decline in network television production values which give cause for concern. This is reflected particularly acutely in some BBC religious television programmes. On Sunday 24 January 1999, the BBC's sole morning offering, *The Heaven and Earth Show*, did not mention anything which could be described as religious until 27 minutes into the hour-long programme. Even then it was an extended trail for that evening's *Songs of Praise*. This was the sole item to represent religion as a positive force. This was no isolated example. Two months later in its television preview column for Sunday 21 March 1999, *The Church of England Newspaper* said of *The Heaven and Earth Show*: 'In today's programme there appears to be no Christian content whatsoever.'

The same paper, three months later on 27 June commented: 'Illustrating this programme's increasingly apparent allergy towards Christianity, the spiritual side of the rock festival at Glastonbury is explored, while chef Michael Barry cooks Muslim food and Mike Harding looks at Zoroastrianism.' Again, on 10 September 1999, the paper suggested: 'Anyone who wants anything relevant to religion would be best advised turning over to channel 3.' The presenters are unimpressive – celebrity chef, Kevin Woodford and former Cadbury's Flake girl, Catrina Skepper. According to Maggie Brown of *The Guardian*, March 1999: '*The Heaven and Earth Show* is lively and topical, but marred by looking like a low budget regional magazine show masquerading as a network programme. Typical topics include Buddhism, food for Passover and the fad for saying "sorry".' The producer, Chris Loughlin admits: 'It's less about religion, more about life' (*The Guardian*, March 1999). The problem is not so much that such programmes are broadcast, but that this one series accounts for somewhere between a third and one half of the total BBC television religious output.

The press criticism continued well into 2000, with Gillean Craig commenting: 'I suppose there is a place for such a programme, aimed at the populace uncontaminated by the virus of faith, but happy enough to be prodded every now and again towards the margins of that foreign land, religious belief and practice: but for this to be our public service network's only Sunday morning programme containing any trace of religion is little short of a public disgrace' (*Church Times*, 12 May 2000).

In marked contrast, ITV's longer Sunday morning coverage seemed to be better produced and presented, and more strongly spiritual in content. As Maggie Brown says:

Resembling holy clones of Richard and Judy are husband and wife presenters, Michael Nesbitt and Linda Bryans. Both possess educated Northern Irish accents. In their secular lives, they jointly present Ulster Television's evening news. Bryans is a practising Christian, a Presbyterian; Nesbitt an agnostic. They've not been selected on religious grounds. Their differences provide a bit of grit. An hour-long magazine format is a big break with tradition, because it acts as a wrapper around a reduced helping of old-fashioned worship. This is the key reason why everyone is extremely twitchy about it, and why once a month ITV is still running a straightforward service.

(*The Guardian*, March 1999)

ITV had carried morning worship for 43 years between 1955 and 1998. At the close it attracted about half a million viewers. ITV in Scotland continues to carry a broadcast service every week. The replacement magazine programme south of the border represented a saving of £7,000 a week on the £28,000 the live outside broadcast had previously cost. The 1990 Broadcasting Act requires ITV to include acts of worship involving the viewer and reflecting the predominant beliefs of the United Kingdom.

The BBC late Sunday offering, *The Big End*, was even more disturbing in nature than the morning show. This was inimical to faith, a deterrent to the younger audience at whom it was aimed (see Appendix D). The series featured, each week, a transsexual nun as its correspondent in the United States of America. Vox pops were also a regular feature and once asked the question: 'Who should lead a new religion?' The consensus favoured Basil Brush.

The Head of BBC Religious Broadcasting, the Reverend Ernie Rea, who has presided over the department throughout the 1990s, was questioned about broadcasting such material. His justification: 'People have stereotypical ideas about religious television and don't think it's for them. The BBC has become more audience-focussed ... *The Big End* looks at some of the weird and wonderful things associated with faith. There are fruitcakes out there who believe God is talking to them because they cut open a potato and see an image of the Virgin. It is all part of the diversity and broadening of the religious agenda on the BBC' (*Broadcast*, 26 March 1999). But should it be?

Meanwhile, the programmes of distinction become fewer. *The Big End* shared the Sunday evening slot which, in 1988, *Heart of the Matter* and *Everyman* occupied for 48 weeks of the year. In 1999/2000, these last two appeared in only 20 weeks. For significant periods of the year there are no BBC religious Sunday evening offerings after six o'clock. When they do appear, it is ever later. *Heart of the Matter* on Palm Sunday 1999, started at 11.45 p.m. and ended the following day at 12.25 a.m. It is no surprise that the audience has fallen, on average, from three million to one million in recent years. This is such a shame as these are the relatively high-budget programmes, though the presenter, Joan Bakewell, when she left at the end of the series in April 2000, pointed out that she felt the BBC had neglected religious broadcasting. *Heart of the Matter,* she said, had been subject to budget cuts year after year and referred to the ever later transmission time as one of the reasons for leaving after twelve years.

The BBC announced at the end of 1999 that *Everyman* would (from 2000) begin no later than 10.40 p.m. In that placing it can attract around three and a half million viewers but now the annual quota of such programmes has been reduced to just twelve a year. It is a pity that the Head of Religious Broadcasting described the audience for such programmes as the 'religious élite'; clearly that is far from being the case. The other concession to the public debate in the General Synod was that the repeat of *Songs of*

Praise, dropped five years ago, is reinstated. Almost forty years after the programme began, it still manages effectively to tell moving stories of faith changing the direction of lives and helping people find hope in adversity.

Concerned licence payers may have felt that the decline of BBC religious coverage appears to have accelerated since the Religious Broadcasting Department was moved out of London to Manchester in 1994. That move was against the advice of the Central Religious Advisory Committee and the Communications Committee of the Church of England, and indeed many members of BBC staff. Several chose not to move, thereby reducing the specialist skills base. The sad consequence is a catalogue of spiritual slippage quite counter to the BBC's repeated public pronouncements. Whether the department would be strengthened by a return to London is a moot point. Much more would seem to depend on the quality of staff and leadership. Head of Entertainment and Features, BBC Manchester, Wayne Garvie said: 'One of the difficulties of running a production centre outside London is that the pool of talent on which you can draw is not very big. At the same time, it is more difficult for those people to find work elsewhere in the north west than it is for those based in London' (BBC staff newspaper, *Ariel*, March 1999). That statement coincided with the loss of 21 production posts from Mr Garvie's department, announced in March 1999. Reorganization means that Religious Broadcasting management in Manchester takes responsibility for programmes that are not considered religious. These include the media affairs programme, *The Message*, as well as non-religious music programmes for Radio 3 such as *100 Great Singers* and *On Air*.

The broadcasting environment had changed at an unprecedented rate in the 1950s and more particularly in the 1960s. A committee under Lord Annan pondered the future of broadcasting and reported to the Government in March 1977. The introduction to Chapter 20 spoke of no arrest in the declining influence of the churches. Nevertheless it went on to say that 'while the churches may be weak, concern about religion is strong … we do not belong to a country where all the springs of religious life have dried up … A large public still speculates about myth and ritual, death and the meaning of life, holiness and evil … Broadcasting has responded to these changes' (*Report of the Committee on the Future of Broadcasting*, HMSO, 1977).

Circumstances are indeed different in the year 2000. But all the statistical evidence suggests that religious broadcasting ought to command significant amounts of airtime at prominent places in the schedules, if there is any commitment to public service. In the late 1980s, *The Good Book*, a 13-part series presented by Brian Redhead, quadrupled the Radio 4 audience for the time slot it was allocated. Earlier in the 1980s, *Priestland's Progress* proved to be highly popular generating twenty-four thousand letters from listeners and much favourable press publicity. *Sunday* built its audience to a level comparable to that achieved by the *Today* programme. Ecumenical initiatives like 'Lent 86' were given broadcast series. A Billy Graham rally was broadcast live on Radio 4. The *BBC Handbook 1986/87* said: 'By every objective test Religious Broadcasting has never been as widely appreciated by its audience as it is today.' At that time 11 million people heard one or more religious radio programmes a week and 8 million watched *Songs of Praise*. *Highway* on ITV drew another 4 million.

The Central Religious Advisory Committee (CRAC) today brings together managers in the broadcasting organizations and sixteen representatives of the Christian churches and other faiths. They are chosen not by the religious bodies but by the BBC and ITC. A CRAC working party presented a report called *Religion in Religious Broadcasting* in November 1996. It maintained that: 'Still the majority associates itself, however loosely, with the religious and cultural heritage of Christianity ... Evangelical Christianity has continued to grow, as have the Christian ecumenical movement and the churches' concern for social justice.'

In 1977, CRAC re-drafted its objectives. Religious broadcasting, it said, should:

1. Seek to reflect the worship, thought and action of the principal religious foundations represented in Britain, recognizing that the traditions are mainly, though not exclusively, Christian;
2. Seek to present to viewers and listeners those beliefs, ideas, issues and experiences in the contemporary world as are evidently related to a religious interpretation or dimension of life;
3. Seek also to meet the religious interests, concerns and needs of those on the fringe of, or outside the organized life of, the churches.

In recent years the BBC, as an organization, has appeared to show less respect for the churches' concerns. The churches need to consider whether they can trust the BBC to fulfil its public service obligations in relation to religion. With debates in the General Synod of the Church of England, at the Methodist Conference and at the Assembly of the United Reformed Church, Christians are beginning to present their case more cogently. The Board of Governors of the BBC appears suddenly to be taking CRAC more seriously. Momentum at a national level must be maintained, for the decline in BBC religious programmes has been exceedingly rapid and needs to be addressed and rectified. The decline has been at odds with the BBC's own research findings and repeated public statements and assurances.

BBC Religion: Programme Strategy Review, written in March 1995, observed that: 'All religious programmes on television represent good value in comparison with light entertainment, factual documentaries, magazines or music and arts programmes embodying similar production values.' Perhaps it is time that the BBC Governors began to take an interest in the mismatch between 'promises' and programmes. There is a precedent. The *BBC Handbook 1978* records in relation to the ending of the 'closed period' that: 'It was our concern to ensure that justice would be done to the religious programme which was to move from its "protected" timing to one later in the evening.' This was the documentary strand. 'One interesting feature was that a sub-group of the Board, consisting of three Governors, made a special study of religious broadcasting and its practitioners within the BBC. Their advice to the rest of the Board was invaluable. It was the fruit of the best kind of relationship between Governors and executive' (*BBC Handbook 1978*).

Then the Central Religious Advisory Committee exerted great influence. It recommended that:

1. There should continue to be at least 70 minutes of religious television on Sunday evenings on BBC 1 and ITV.
2. Thirty-five minutes of this output should be screened at the same time on BBC 1 and ITV terminating together, if possible, at 7.15 p.m.
3. The Committee supported the declared proposal of the BBC to schedule *Anno Domini* or future comparable programmes at 10.15 p.m.

4. The Committee supported the declared proposals of ITV to continue its output in one 70-minute period. The Committee would prefer this to be from 6.05 p.m. to 7.15 p.m. with the option of occasionally moving the earlier part of that output to between 4.00 p.m. and 6.05 p.m.

5. The Committee welcomed the assurance from the BBC that BBC 2 programming between 6.05 p.m. and 7.15 p.m. would be of a similar kind to that previously broadcast at that time, and understood that BBC 1 would replace the religious programming previously carried in the earlier part of the former 'closed period' with family-type viewing.

These recommendations were accepted both by the BBC and the IBA and the changes in the timings of the BBC programmes took place in April 1977.

In those days CRAC was able to achieve results, though there was disquiet about its composition as far back as 1973. In that year the Church of England Broadcasting Commission Report, *Broadcasting, Society and the Church*, recommended that because CRAC is often regarded as speaking for the churches but is appointed by the broadcasters, 'one-third of its membership should be appointed by the churches. Those from the Church of England should be appointed by the General Synod. CRAC should either meet more frequently or delegate to sub-committees, with a view to giving more detailed consideration to policy and programmes.' In the House of Commons in October 1999, Desmond Swayne called for an end to the broadcasters' control over appointments to CRAC.

In the General Synod debate of February 2000, the present Chairman, the Archbishop of York, said:

I am entirely at ease with the suggestion Mr Holmes makes that 'the future function of CRAC should be assessed'. Indeed, since becoming Chairman that is something I have been seeking to do and hopefully to some effect. However, I am mindful that the Committee does work within formal terms of reference which make it very clear that the Committee is an advisory body – 'CRAC's opinion may be sought on the understanding that it has no powers to tell the broadcasting bodies what they may or may not do'. However, 'CRAC may choose to act as a pressure group, bringing its influence to bear on the appropriate authorities'.

(Proceedings of the General Synod of the Church of England, February 2000)

He went on to hope that 'the relationship between CRAC and the BBC Governors might become more in line with the relationship we have with the ITC where CRAC prepares an annual report and that report is presented by the Chairman personally to the ITC'. At the first meeting of CRAC following the Synod debate, the BBC promised that some Governors would, unusually, be attending.

As we have seen, CRAC is still active, if less effective than it was in the 1970s. Its working party report, entitled *Religion in Religious Broadcasting* in November 1996, discerned the beginnings of marginalization of such output within the schedules.

Religious Broadcasting is, of course, subject to the decision-making of schedulers, and religious programmes are sometimes positioned in ways which do not enhance their status or audience. This must demoralise those concerned and may be discouraging some talented programme-makers from involvement with Religious Broadcasting. Colleagues in other sectors may gain the impression that religion and Religious Broadcasting are of little concern, of minority interest and perhaps even anachronistic. But an appreciation of the cultural, historical and contemporary significance of religion, and a well-informed approach to matters related to religion, should be a professional requisite across the field of broadcasting.

(*Religion in Religious Broadcasting*, CRAC, 1996)

That CRAC report called on the broadcasters 'to take seriously and build upon people's quest for meaning, for the well-being (shalom) of society. Religious Broadcasting can help to do this, as part of its function of educating, informing and reflecting.' This seems to have fallen on deaf ears since the report's publication. Elsewhere that report says: 'Broadcasters have tried to represent the phenomena of religion and its concerns, the spiritual search and the effects in our world of belief and unbelief, in ways which do not sensationalise, do not concentrate unduly on the marginal and the provocative, and which do not assume (wrongly) the triumph of secularism' (*Religion in Religious Broadcasting*, CRAC, 1996). The authors would not have approved of much BBC television output on 24 January 1999 (see Appendix D).

In the General Synod Debate, the Chairman of CRAC, the Archbishop of York, challenged the observations of William Phillips:

With nary a squeak from the Central Religious Advisory Committee, *Songs of Praise* [in 1998] drifted back to a 5.30–6.00 p.m. slot. CRAC, an unwieldy multi-faith convocation of more than twenty divines [the number should read sixteen] which rarely meets, has rubber-stamped every cutback. The oft-reiterated justification for purging religion from the main channels are at best half-truths. The fall in church attendance was halted, if not reversed, some years ago. Newer brands of Christianity are recruiting rapidly and the broadcasters' mania for multi-culturalism conspicuously excludes regular presentation of the flourishing black churches, let alone Muslim or Hindu rites.

(*Broadcast*, 26 March 1999)

It should be noted that the Sikh religion attracted coverage in 1999 from the BBC on the 300th anniversary of the Khalsa. The Corporation invited senior figures from the Sikh community to the Council Chamber in Broadcasting House 'for a celebration to mark this special time for the community and in recognition of its importance to the UK'. Then the BBC covered the Sikh festival Vaisakhi for the first time. Historically, the BBC has given better coverage than other broadcasters to religions other than Christianity. In 1984, the children's programme *Knock, Knock* told religious stories from a variety of faiths, and in the summer of the same year *Encounters with Islam* presented reflections from Muslim scholars. In the late 1980s there were several series of *Umbrella*, a multi-faith story-telling programme for children. BBC Education has long produced programmes about other faiths. A major such series to be transmitted in 2001 is called *Pathways of Belief*. In 2000, the BBC held a seminar on Islam, organized by the new BBC Diversity Centre, to explain what programme-makers can do to broaden the contribution of Muslims to mainstream output. The producer who organized the seminar, Navid Akhtar, explained in the BBC Equality newsletter: 'There have been so many changes in the British Muslim community in the last ten years, particularly after the Rushdie affair. Many young Muslims now identify more fully with their faith and see themselves as British Muslims, rather than Asians' (*BBC Equality Newsletter*, May 2000).

4

The End of BBC Religious Broadcasting

In comes BBC Faith and Identity – or Culture – or Spirituality

It's generally agreed that the BBC was caught with its pants down when Nigel Holmes was able to quote from the BBC's own figures to argue his case that religious programmes were being marginalised at the BBC.

(BBC Religious Broadcasting staff bulletin, April 2000)

'A religious broadcasting department justifies its separate existence in the last resort because its subject matter is religious faith – what it is, what it does and what its consequences are ... One assumption is that religious faith has its source in some transcendent power. The second is that it embraces not just Christianity but any expression of faith which acknowledges the transcendent.' So said Colin Morris in *God-in-a-Box*, which he wrote whilst Head of BBC Religious Television in 1984. He went on to enumerate the various forms of religious broadcasting – exploration, teaching, argument, worship, meditation and reflection. Worship he regarded as the 'lynchpin' of the output of a religious broadcasting department. 'Other areas may be more topical, popular or generally significant, but they are derivative because they take as read the issue which worship tackles head on.' In Colin Morris's day there was regular worship on BBC Television, now seen only at festivals. There is a ferment of change and changing perceptions of the context of religious broadcasting in which worship appears ever more at the periphery.

The overriding theme of the strategy document *BBC Religion – Into the Third Millennium,* issued by the Head of Religious Broadcasting, the Reverend Ernie Rea, in June 1999, is the coverage of faiths other than Christianity. The language used was felt by some staff to be threatening. 'If BBC Religion is to succeed, all of us, at every level, must change ... We'll all have to act, all the time, in line with the values, mission, and strategy of the Department, and of individual strands' (*BBC Religion – Into the Third Millennium,* June 1999). The tenor of the document is that there must be marked change from proclaiming faith first and foremost from a Christian perspective. One section is entitled 'Strategy for a multi-faith world':

> Many people think BBC Religion looks rooted in Western Christianity with occasional other faith output. This isn't true of our documentaries or our talk and debate output, but is the result of the volume of quasi-worship Christian output that we make, which is all some people regard as real religious programming. Statistics show that Christianity (and Judaism) is losing active members while minority faiths are growing and that New Age and activities with rather vague faith elements are booming.
>
> (*BBC Religion – Into the Third Millennium,* June 1999)

Where does this thinking leave *Songs of Praise* and the *Daily Service*?

One could be forgiven for sensing that this document has the not-so-hidden agenda of disposing of the principles behind public service religious broadcasting, which have not been ashamed to recognize the importance, both past and present, of the Christian faith in this country. The impression given is that some in positions of influence now find these principles deeply embarrassing, even though their own figures list 6 million active Christians, almost ten times the number of active Muslims. However, few would dispute that more than 35 million Britons have Christian affiliations and that membership of all non-Christian faiths amounts to no more than five per cent of the population of the United Kingdom. The whole thread through the document stresses the importance of recruiting people with knowledge of other faiths and ensuring that Christians on the staff play down their areas of specialist knowledge, expertise and understanding, so as to appear to be in line with the declared strategy. The present workforce is criticized for producing programmes with a dull image, being too Christian, establishment and middle class and 'somewhat demoralised and battered'.

> General conclusions of the strategy – we will broaden our scope. BBC Religion will adapt itself to cater for the modern world's spiritual values and needs. We will help the BBC to adapt itself too. We'll do this by taking the wider view of the religious subject area ... BBC Religion will be a truly multi-faith department and a champion of 'The Many Faces of Britain'. We will assist the BBC to provide a better service to faith groups and communities.
>
> (*BBC Religion – Into the Third Millennium*, June 1999)

The cover of the document is dominated by 13 pictures from faiths other than Christianity and even incorporates one showing members of the Ku Klux Klan.

The stream of support for the self-declared multi-faith mission the BBC is espousing is so much at the heart of this strategy that the Religious Broadcasting Department proposes to 'link to the multicultural studies and cross-cultural perspectives programme at Manchester Metropolitan University', give 'minority faith subjects a high priority in setting staff development objectives ... appoint an in-house champion for each minority faith' and advertise 'Staff Posts ... in minority community papers' (*BBC Religion – Into the Third Millennium*, June 1999). It cannot be long until Christian worship programmes are being produced by non-Christians. Further, it could be argued that the Christian influence through the Central Religious Advisory Committee would be further weakened by the intention of 'creating an informal team of advisors from the faith communities of Manchester. They will be expert, approachable, accessible and available' and 'will give a number of seminars each year to brief staff on particular faiths and inform about current issues' (*BBC Religion – Into the Third Millennium*, June 1999).

This document seems driven by the direction in which BBC Religious Broadcasting perceives the Corporate Centre of the BBC wants it to go. There is no attempt to present the achievements of the past as a fine base from which to build. All is to change. Some change would appear desirable, for there is much confession of failure, particularly in relation to the management of staff. Yet those very staff do not know what is in prospect for them. They do not know what is meant by their having to become 'champions of different faiths'. Many are motivated by their Christian faith and see their work in broadcasting as a vocation. They find no theological justification for what is now placed before them. Many skilled and talented specialists in this field were lost as a result of the move to Manchester seven years ago. Those who did move felt that they had been separated from the heartland of creative production. If this policy is implemented, the remaining critical core of creativity in this field could finally be dispersed. In the 1980s, one of the managerial maxims was 'where's religion in this programme?'; now nobody asks that question.

The document neatly sidesteps the BBC's own *Statement of Promises* published in 1996, which sought to target serious religious output at young people. This has never materialized. The implication is that these promises no longer matter, for the 'markets where we will sell our output' significantly do not mention either Radio 1 or Radio 5 Live.

There is the assertion that 'The high status that the BBC gives Religion and religious output is a daily reminder of the BBC's public service values' (*BBC Religion – Into the Third Millennium*, June 1999). This ignores the fact that, on the Corporation's own figures, in the ten years between 1987/88 and 1997/98 BBC television analogue terrestrial output has increased by a half, whereas BBC television religious output has declined by a third and none appears regularly in peak time. What is more, there is no regular religious output on the two new public service digital channels, BBC Choice and BBC Knowledge. In radio, 1998/99 was unprecedented in seeing both marginalization of much output and a 15 per cent fall in the hours of religion broadcast. So then to assert that these public service values 'reinforce the argument for the unique way in which the BBC is funded, by demonstrating the Corporation's substantial commitment to important output areas that the free market would treat only in a token way' is absurd.

The BBC must be challenged about such misleading statements. It is interesting that the authors of this document contradict facts from published BBC sources when they say: 'Some channels already take so much religious output as returning strands that commissioners don't want to buy more.' It also reveals the degree to which subjectivity is evident within the commissioning process. 'Some [commissioners] have a narrow view of what religious programming could be, and are cool to religious output.' Was this the reason for the dramatic fall in programmes carried by BBC 2? Hope is expressed that the Department could develop an ancient history strand for BBC 2. The report continues: 'The job of the management team of Religious Broadcasting is to "learn the likes and dislikes" of commissioners' (*BBC Religion – Into the Third Millennium*, June 1999). In 1999, the Department took responsibility for some radio output of a non-religious nature for Radio 3 and Radio 4.

The publication of this document has heightened the atmosphere of distrust and fear. All the executive producers have put their names to the strategy, so it is difficult for producers and other staff to question the thinking behind a strategy devised over two years with little departmental consultation. Those staff harbour serious concerns about the direction in which this policy would lead BBC Religious Broadcasting but are afraid to articulate them for fear of jeopardizing their own jobs.

Less than a year later in April 2000, following the publicity associated with my Private Member's Motion in the General Synod of the Church of England, the bulletin of the BBC Religious Broadcasting Department declared that:

> Yes folks, there is a new religion strategy underway. But this time it's not all about us. It's generally agreed that the BBC was caught with its pants down when Nigel Holmes was able to quote from the BBC's own figures to argue his case that religious programmes were being marginalised at the

BBC. The problem was that the BBC's figures were based entirely on the output of this Department. *The Sikhs* (TV), *St. Paul's* (TV) and *Something Understood* (radio) were left out because they're Indies [independent producers' originations].

(BBC Religious Broadcasting staff bulletin, April 2000)

However, these two television series were broadcast in the year 1999/2000, following that for which I quoted output statistics. In total, they would amount to about five hours less in a year, hardly a blip when religious output fell by 65 hours within the ten years from 1987/88 to 1997/98 whilst total hours of output on BBC 1 and BBC 2 increased by 50 per cent. Likewise, the inclusion of *Something Understood* would make a negligible difference as it was reduced in length from 50 to 30 minutes in 1998 and rescheduled from 6.05 a.m. to 6.35 a.m.

The bulletin continued:

The Synod debate has brought into sharp focus the difficult issue of how the BBC should address the whole issue of religious broadcasting provision in the new millennium. So Ernie [Rea, Head of the Department] has been invited to write a draft strategy paper on how the BBC should tackle the provision of religious programmes across all platforms: TV, radio and online. And we've got our own red hot broadcast strategist to help us ... She's on our side. The final strategy must be one that can be monitored properly so that the BBC can produce figures to demonstrate that it is dealing properly, fairly and responsibly with this 'life area'. It also has to be a strategy which commissioners will buy into and that can overcome the hostile reception given to religious content in some BBC areas ... One quick way of demonstrating the wider range of topics that religious broadcasting should cover is to change the name of this department. The aim is to find a broader title that doesn't abandon the core subject. Should the word 'religion' stay in our title? Names in the frame already: Faith and Identity, Faith and Culture, Faith and Society, Faith Values and Culture, Faith and Values, Faith and Spirituality.

(BBC Religious Broadcasting staff bulletin, April 2000)

In July 2000, the Director-General announced that he had chosen the title 'Religious Affairs and Ethics' and the head of this area 'would sit above the present role of Head of Religion'. Greg Dyke was quoted as saying, 'A lot of research we've done suggests that there are many people who are interested in spirituality today, who are not particularly interested in formal religion. That isn't to say we are going to ban formal religion, because we are not. Actually it's an attempt to re-stimulate religious programming on television.'

(*The Guardian*, 11 July 2000)

5

Standards of Integrity

Churches to keep broadcasters accountable

A mechanism for monitoring the provision and quality of religious programmes in the future would send out a signal to all broadcasters that we are taking this matter very seriously and systematically.

(The Right Reverend Nigel McCulloch, Bishop of Wakefield, February 2000)

Vigilance over standards will become ever more critical, as the digital revolution forces producers to cut corners in seeking to adjust to ever lower budgets. Integrity of output is at risk as the deceptions within the BBC's *Vanessa* and ITV's *Trisha* chat shows demonstrated. The presenter of the Radio 4 *Sunday* programme, Roger Bolton, wrote at the time:

What has gone wrong? A BBC news report rather disingenuously suggested that the real worry was what was happening with independents, conveniently ignoring the fact that *Vanessa* is an in-house production and *Trisha* is produced by Anglia TV. It looked like a rather lame and disreputable attempt to deflect blame. I think the recent scandals have been caused first by the drive to make some TV journalism primarily entertainment, and second by ruthless budget-cutting and the casualisation of the industry ... Young, inexperienced researchers are being exploited and then reviled. What is the way out of this mess? First: The broadcasters, primarily the BBC, should call a halt to this downward spiral in the sensationalism stakes. Second: They should acknowledge that culling of staff has gone too far and fix more realistic budgets ... At the moment too many of them appear to be auditioning for the part of Pontius Pilate, washing their hands of a problem they have largely created.

(*The Guardian*, 1999)

Lord Holme, Deputy Chairman of the Independent Television Commission, sought to define 'public service':

I identify the following elements in varying degrees, which both the BBC and the main commercial channels share. They all have some requirement for impartiality and a balanced fairness of some sort, particularly in their reporting of contentious issues. I am sure they all accept that there is some need for authority, responsibility, and verisimilitude in what they do. Interestingly, some of the cases on which the ITC had to regulate recently had to do with the simulation or faking of scenes. The concept that it is important to know that what we watch is the real thing is part of the notion of authority and responsibility.

(Lord Holme, debate on 'Public Service Broadcasting', House of Lords, 5 May 1999)

It is crucial for religious broadcasting that programmes are produced by those whose integrity is undoubted and who possess specialist knowledge and understanding of their field. Lord Phillips spoke in the same debate of the increasing commercialization of broadcasting during the past ten years:

I refer not merely to the growth of commercial companies, but to the growth of huge, immensely powerful global corporations with no fixed loyalty, run by individuals who, without ascribing to them either ill will or malice, are interested in dominance and profit and precious little else. It behoves us to look that reality fairly and squarely in the eye. Maintenance of quality and standards in broadcasting against a background of overweening preoccupation with capital and income profit is extremely difficult to achieve ... This debate provides an opportunity to express a certain anxiety as to the degree to which the BBC is today maintaining the best traditions of its inheritance.

(Lord Phillips, debate on 'Public Service Broadcasting', House of Lords, 5 May 1999)

He went on to express concern about the marginalization of certain areas of output. This is one reason why I proposed in a background paper for the General Synod debate that the churches needed to organize systematic monitoring both of the content and placing of religious programmes, particularly on television. The Synod agreed to this and referred the matter to the Archbishops' Council for implementation during 2000.

It is time for the churches to emulate other groups in society which feel that their interests are being marginalized by the BBC. The farming and countryside lobby has attracted much attention. The Editor of *Country Life*, Clive Aslet, wrote:

The media – that is metropolitan to the last luvvie. One would have expected the BBC, with its Reithian respect for balance, to act as a corrective. Instead it reinforces the prejudice. Try listening to Radio 4 of an evening. You will hear programmes for every kind of minority, but traditional country dwellers are the one minority whom it is politically correct to ignore. Far from trying to remedy this state of affairs, BBC executives have striven to make it worse. Real country programmes have been cut and rescheduled for times when nobody can hear them.

(*Country Life*, 1999)

When John Birt was appointed Director-General without anyone else having the opportunity to apply, John Tusa, then in charge of the World Service, was effectively passed over. To many staff he was the best candidate for the job. He is now Head of the Barbican Centre in London. At Easter 2000, he criticized BBC television's coverage of classical music. Writing in *The Independent*, he said:

It is not just about the quantity of classical music programming on television that has declined, though the fall is real enough. A decade ago, say insiders, the BBC was broadcasting 100 hours per year. Now we are down to just half that number. The more serious collapse is of true commitment to the very idea of sustained coverage of classical music. A decade ago, a proposed *Omnibus* on Simon Rattle – Britain's finest conductor and one of the top handful of world-class conductors – would have been a prize; today it is rejected because he is regarded by TV planners as of 'insufficient popular interest' ... What is it with British TV schedulers? These programmes find homes and slots on European television. Why not here? ... The charge is that there is far less in quantity and that TV controllers no longer believe that it matters ... I have always maintained to those searching for signs of a bright, post-Birt BBC, that Dyke would be put to the test over classical music.

(*The Independent*, April 2000)

Religion and classical music are the only two categories of BBC television programme that have no regular broadcast in peak time.

Christians, like country-dwellers and those who enjoy classical music, seem to be fewer amongst the schedulers and producers of London W1 and W12, than in the population of the country at large. Yet the churches are represented in every community and, given a lead, could mount a well-organized lobby that would exert considerable influence. It is increasingly important that Christians take the inroads to influence which are now open to application, including the Board of Governors of the BBC. Church leaders can no longer take for granted a fair share of appointees to the most powerful broadcasting bodies. There has been no member of the clergy on the Board of Governors since the Church of Scotland minister, Norman Drummond, stepped down in 1998. The churches' appointments committees need to identify and encourage those who might be regarded as strong candidates by the Department of Culture, Media and Sport. Interestingly, religion is part of the portfolio of this Department.

At the conference of the Churches' Advisory Council for Local Broadcasting in 1999, I floated the idea of some kind of low cost systematic monitoring of network religious output, both quantitative and qualitative, so that never again could so much be lost so speedily with barely a murmur of regret from the churches' official spokesmen/ women. My suggestion prompted one of those, the Church of England's media voice in the House of Lords, Nigel McCulloch, Bishop of Wakefield, to 'call the churches to arms' over this issue. In the General Synod debate he said:

A mechanism for monitoring the provision and quality of religious programmes in the future would send out a signal to all broadcasters that we are taking this matter very seriously and systematically. This is not to diminish the significance of CRAC [Central Religious Advisory Committee], but that body is part of the broadcasters' own mechanism. My amendment asks the Archbishops' Council to develop this mechanism independently from the BBC and commercial sectors. Such a monitoring body, with co-operation from other churches and interested bodies, knowing who is broad-casting what and when, would lead to regular tabled qualitative as well as quantitative assessments. These would offer a 'health-check' on religious broadcasting, which I believe we need, and inform in an intelligent way general public debate.

(Proceedings of the General Synod of the Church of England, 29 February 2000)

Christians need to act to ensure that their faith is not ridiculed, marginalized, or summarily and deliberately dumped by the BBC. Hitherto, the churches have assumed that good would prevail in Broadcasting House, the foyer of which is dominated by the dedication 'DEO OMNIPOTENTI' and the words of Philippians 4:8: 'Whatsoever things are true, whatsoever things are honest, whatsoever things are just, whatsoever things are pure, whatsoever things are lovely, whatsoever things are of good report; if there be any virtue, and if there be any praise, think on these things.' So how does the BBC see its mission at the turn of the millennium?

Today's BBC is moving confidently forward into the new world of digital broadcasting. Our plans and ambitions are carefully considered and we are already launching new services and making new alliances. But as the trustees for the public interest in the BBC, the Board of Governors will ensure that standards and values are maintained and that the BBC continues to be a public service, universally available. It is, and will remain, your BBC.

(The Chairman, Sir Christopher Bland, *BBC Annual Report 1997/98*)

We believe that the BBC is getting much better at listening to audiences and hearing what they are saying about programmes – but there is more that can be done. Over a four-year cycle every aspect of BBC programming is reviewed from the point of view of the audience. This year (1997/98) we considered listening reports on children's programmes, daily news, political programmes, consumer and leisure, religious broadcasting and programmes for schools.

('The BBC Listens', *Annual Report 1997/98*)

We aim to be the world's most creative and trusted broadcaster and programme-maker, seeking to satisfy all our audiences in the UK with services that inform, educate and entertain and that enrich their lives in ways that the market alone will not. We aim to be guided by our public purposes; to encourage the UK's most innovative talents; to act independently of all interests; to aspire to the highest ethical standards; to offer the best value for money; to be accountable to our licence-payers; to endeavour to be the world's leading international broadcaster; and to be the best – or to learn from the best – in everything we do.

(*The BBC Beyond 2000*, December 1998)

6

A National Debate Begins
Unprecedented media attention

> Television is one of the most powerful of the principalities
> and powers – those secular institutions which are not under
> the churches' thumb but still within the range of God's
> sovereignty. It is by wrestling with principalities and power
> that Christians achieve true spiritual maturity.
>
> (The Reverend Colin Morris, former Head of BBC
> Religious Television, *God-in-a-Box*, 1984)

In October 1999, the BBC organized its first general listener and viewer consultation exercise by telephone and
internet contact. The booklet distributed, *BBC 2000 and
Beyond – What's Your View?*, included a questionnaire
which asked people to indicate the types of programmes
they watch. There were a dozen categories, from soaps to
regional programmes. Yet there was no reference to religion and no space to indicate 'other' genre.

One reason why religious broadcasting has not thrived
in the BBC in recent years is this very word *genre*, according to Jayne Ozanne, a member of the Archbishops'
Council who, a few years ago, handled marketing for BBC
channel controllers. In the General Synod she pointed out
that all the BBC's planning, debate, reviews and research
now focused on genres: groups of programmes which all

had the same style such as drama, entertainment, sport, news, music, etc. But religious broadcasting is not classed by the BBC as a genre. 'There is therefore very little focus at a central level on religion, no central objectives are set for it and therefore there is no end-of-year measure and thus no central accountability.' She concluded: 'Until this changes, there will I predict be little noticeable change to religious broadcasting within the BBC' (General Synod of the Church of England, 29 February 2000).

But Roger Bolton, independent producer and presenter of *Sunday* on Radio 4, writing in a personal capacity in *The Tablet*, issued a call for change: 'Everyone interested in improving the range, volume and quality of religious broadcasting should exert every means of pressure possible on those who commission the BBC programmes' (*The Tablet*, 13 November 1999).

I think I can fairly claim to have initiated that national debate in July 1999, four months before Roger Bolton wrote that article. His article was prompted by 'A Symposium on Religious Broadcasting' which the BBC held in late October, chaired by Baroness Young, Vice-chairman of the BBC Governors. Mark Thompson, then Director of National and Regional Broadcasting, now Director of BBC Television, reiterated the BBC's commitment to religion but did admit that mistakes had been made, citing Christmas 1998 and the ever later placing of those twenty serious religious programmes a year which have survived. He spoke of the need for the BBC to be more consistent. He stressed the growth of 'free-form spirituality' as mainstream Christian faith continued to decline and articulated his concern about the BBC appearing to promote superstition but felt that religious broadcasting had to be more 'open to change'. This also appeared to imply better coverage for minority faiths: 'We can do more for other faiths at the same time as clarifying a commitment to Christianity' (BBC Religious Broadcasting Symposium, October 1999).

Gavin Drake, Senior Communications Officer for the Evangelical Alliance, felt that the number invited to attend the symposium from minority faiths provided an imbalance of representation. Muslim voices called for the BBC to provide a weekly act of Islamic worship on Fridays as an acknowledgement that Islam is the second religion in Britain. Afterwards Gavin Drake wrote:

> Their plea sounded plausible until you look at the statistics that show that a Christian disposition can be found in 65 per cent of the population, while the other religious groups account together for 7 per cent. While the BBC needs to acknowledge the presence of other faiths in the UK, an attempt to provide something for everybody will lead to a watering down of the current broadly Christian basis for religious broadcasting, as can already be seen with *The Heaven and Earth Show.*
>
> (BBC Religious Broadcasting Symposium, October 1999)

The Head of Religious Broadcasting, Ernie Rea, referred to this type of programme when he described 'the changing landscape of religious broadcasting', which 'must not be afraid to be popular'. He also wanted 'religious broadcasting to tap into other areas of BBC production'. Lorraine Heggessey, then Director of Programmes, agreed that 'spirituality is part of the fabric of our viewers' lives and this should be reflected in our programmes' (BBC Religious Broadcasting Symposium, October 1999).

Judith Lampard, Administration Officer, Churches Together in England, said: 'The practice of allotting late night slots to religious programmes, assuming that they would be of interest to a minority of viewers was criticized. This ignores the significant number of people who, when answering surveys, claim while not being regular churchgoers to have some experience of faith' (*Crosstalk*, Churches Advisory Council for Local Broadcasting (CACLB), November 1999). Dr Jim McDonnell, Director, Catholic Communications Centre, reckoned that the most important fact about the symposium was that it took place – 'recognition that there are concerns about BBC religion which need to be addressed' (*Crosstalk*, CACLB, November 1999).

Three days after that symposium, on 29 October 1999, the House of Commons held its second debate of the year on broadcasting during which Desmond Swayne quoted the figures I had produced earlier in the year. He went on to say: 'There has been a huge reduction in the total output of religious programmes and in the amount of prime time devoted to such programmes.' He spoke of the omission of religion from both the *BBC Annual Report 1998/99* and 'the document entitled *2000 and Beyond*'. He said he felt it 'entirely inappropriate for the BBC to have any role in the regulation of religious broadcasting. We should remove BBC control over the appointments to the secretariat of CRAC, which should be entirely independent' (*Hansard*, 29 October 1999). He urged the Minister to address that point.

The most significant theme of that debate for the future hinged on regulation. The Secretary of State for Culture, Media and Sport, Chris Smith, said:

We are working with the ITC to examine how regulation in the short term can be simplified and applied more lightly ... I have taken the view shared by the industry that an evolutionary approach to broadcasting regulation is right and broadly sustainable for the time being. However, it is clear to me that the time for a more fundamental assessment of broadcasting regulation is coming and I anticipate that we may be able to include major broadcasting legislation early in the next Parliament. The main issues for such a piece of legislation might be the role of the regulators, the role of public service broadcasters and media ownership. I want to proceed with that work without delay.

(*Hansard*, 29 October 1999)

A dedicated unit was established to prepare a consultation paper. The Opposition spokesman, Peter Ainsworth, said:

A good starting point would be to aim to make the next Broadcasting Bill the last for a considerable time. As the purpose of successive broadcasting acts has been to deregulate, that would mean taking deregulation as far as it will go. Subject to normal competition policy, we should let the market decide the future shape of competition policy. We should let the market decide the future shape of the commercial broadcasting industry.

(*Hansard*, 29 October 1999)

He went on to express the view that 'broadcasting is too important to be left to the politicians' begging the question as to who should possess ultimate control if not the elected representatives of the people. Peter Ainsworth and Chris Smith both believe that the role of the BBC as 'providing a benchmark of quality to which all other broadcasters aspire' is likely in future to grow in importance.

As we have seen, in many respects today, it is the commercial broadcasters who are the religious innovators. To a significant degree, they are setting the benchmark of creativity in this field. Regulation has for almost half a century ensured the presence of religion on ITV and more recently also on Channels 4 and 5. It is therefore disturbing to hear both main political parties assuming that the quality of BBC output would be such, in the post-deregulation future, as to ensure that commercial broadcasters attain similar high standards. This seems to imply that they would be happy to reduce regulatory requirements. Three months later, the Culture Secretary did indeed announce a forthcoming consultation exercise to be held in the autumn of 2000. *The Guardian* reported:

> Rules on programme content, the remit of public service broadcasting and the laws restricting ownership of media companies will all be covered in the White Paper. The terrestrial broadcasters, including ITV, Channel 4 and Channel 5, have long argued for a relaxation of the detailed regulations which govern their programmes and which currently force them to show a certain number of hours of arts, current affairs, children's and religious shows a week. Although Mr Smith has said he aims for a 'lighter touch' regulation of television channels now that digital television has greatly increased the number of channels available, he insisted that viewers' and consumers' interests would be fully protected.
>
> (*The Guardian*, 2 February 2000)

Christians will need to respond to the White Paper to ensure that religious broadcasting is enriched rather than diminished. The public service element must be maintained as a part of the broadcasting ethos both in the BBC and commercial television (which is now controlled by a few large media companies). A balance in the ecology of broadcasting between the two must be maintained for the benefit of the listener and viewer. Throughout the world public service broadcasters are facing increased commercial competition. The consultants McKinsey, commissioned by the BBC a year or so ago, found that in Australia and America the public service corporations have been driven into a low audience ghetto. Unfettered deregulated commercial competition does not best serve the audience, for the alternative to the low audience is to compete directly, as has happened in Italy, but that leads to a sameness of output, largely sport and entertainment, and very few stimulating programmes with high production values.

The other danger is that some will argue that in a multichannel age, it would be far better to siphon off religious programmes to a dedicated digital channel; what could be described as marginalization to the multi-faith ghetto. The Head of BBC Religious Broadcasting, Ernie Rea, alluded to this in his lecture *Faith in the Future* at Manchester University. On the one hand, he said such a channel 'would undermine the whole concept of public service broadcasting if we were to ghettoise existing passions and interests', but on the other hand, 'we should not dismiss an additional *Faith and Cultures* channel. It would surely carry religious programming of all faiths and spiritual interests ... and it is surely worth the BBC taking one of its digital channels and turning it into a multi-faith, multichannel, multi-lingual home for the cultures that now play such a vital role in our country' (*Church of England Newspaper*, 12 November 1999). It is hard to see, on the experience of the recent past at the BBC, how such a channel could be sufficiently well funded in order to maintain high quality worthwhile programmes. At present, there are satellite Christian television channels of a commercial kind, such as *The Dream Family Network*, which originates in Gateshead. This subscription group of channels, transmitted by satellite, was launched in December 1999 with *The God Channel* – films, documentaries, live action, cartoons, Christian music and news, and comment; *The Revival Channel* – teaching, preaching and conferences; *The Worship Channel* – 'breathtaking landscapes and uplifting music to enrich the soul'. *The Dream Family Network* describes its output as 'the broadcasting revolution you've been waiting for. It's 21st century entertainment at its best – and its safest – for Christian families who care about what they watch and what they listen to … A round the clock alternative of programming that reinforces your Christian values and offers wholesome entertainment at the same time … It's igniting a revolution in the British broadcasting arena … You can't afford to be without it at only 43 pence a day' (*Dream Family Network* leaflet, December 1999).

The service is expected soon to include a Christian music radio station, *The Dream*, and claims to be 'Europe's first Christian multi-channel'. *Dream Kids* and *Dream Shopping* are in prospect as future television channels. The organizers would not give figures for the number of subscriptions taken out in the first six months.

The Department for Culture, Media and Sport consultation will also provide a chance for religious organizations to lobby for digital radio and national analogue radio licences, which at present are denied them by law. The Broadcasting Act 1990 prevents religious broadcasters from having anything transmitted from the ground, as opposed to satellite, other than a local radio analogue signal. There is strong competition for such licences and so far only one has been awarded, to Premier in London for medium wave (AM) transmissions only. No frequency modulated (FM) station run by a religious group has been allowed other than under the very limited Restricted Service Licence (RSL). The Broadcasting Act 1996 further limited religious ownership with the advent of digital radio preventing such bodies from obtaining even a local licence. According to Desmond Swayne, MP: 'Religious broadcasting is flourishing in Europe, but the practical effect of our [British] policy is to ban all religious [digital] output, Christian and other. That is a clear breach of the liberty of freedom of speech. David Pannick, QC, has given the opinion that our law breaches the European convention on human rights' (*Hansard*, 29 October 1999).

Many thousands of people have written in support of United Christian Broadcasters (UCB), who are seeking to change the law to allow them to compete for a national terrestrial radio licence. At present, religious organizations can bid only for local radio licences like that gained by Premier Radio to broadcast on medium wave to Greater London. Interestingly, UCB has adopted, as their publicity material puts it, 'the original BBC aims for religious broadcasting'. These are listed as:

> To maintain standards of truth, justice and honesty in private and public life; to explain what the Christian faith is, to remove misunderstanding of it and to demonstrate its relevance for today; to lead non-churchgoers to see that any real Christian commitment involves active membership of a church congregation, while at the same time giving churchgoers a wider vision of what church membership involves; to provide opportunities for that challenge to personal faith in Jesus Christ as Saviour and Lord, which is at the heart of 'conversion'.
>
> (*The Word for Today*, UCB Europe)

From modest beginnings on Manx Radio in the evenings in the 1980s, UCB now broadcasts around the clock from the Astra satellite. UCB Europe, on the air 24 hours a day, is 70 per cent music, 30 per cent speech, the latter including testimonies, interviews, Christian news and 'phone-ins. UCB Cross Rhythms, launched in July 1998, has an 80 per cent music content and also presents Bible teaching aimed at younger listeners. Bible readings are given on the hour, most hours and the stations have since April 1994 produced their own Bible study booklets, *The Word for Today*, from their base at Stoke-on-Trent. The Minister for Broadcasting, Janet Anderson, visited UCB in the autumn of 1999 to hear their case and she said subsequently in the House of Commons that the Government had promised to consider the issue of changing primary legislation 'when the time comes', to allow Christian groups to bid for just such a licence.

That legislation promised for the next Parliament will also have major consequences for the BBC if, as seems likely, it will question the self-governing regulation of the BBC through its Board of Governors. That is another reason why, at present, it is important to keep religious broadcasting publicly to the fore. The chord which this public debate in press and broadcasting has struck has resulted in an unprecedented number of letters and petitions being sent by individuals and churches to the Board of Governors.

It is vital that pressure is maintained, for as Roger Bolton said in *The Tablet*:

> Religious broadcasting has to broaden its agenda and have a larger place in the country's agenda. Only once in a decade is there a patch of blue sky to aim at, a moment when a strategic shift in BBC priorities is possible. I believe this is one of those moments. There is a new Director-General and a fresh debate about the BBC's public service role is taking place, encouraged by an enlightened government minister, Chris Smith. Everyone interested in improving the range, volume and quality of religious broadcasting should exert every means of pressure possible on those who commission the BBC programmes. They might just listen.
>
> (*The Tablet*, 13 November 1999)

7

The BBC's Digital Policy

Religious Niche Lost in a Cultural Cul-de-Sac?

If the BBC's main purpose is to copy what commercial broadcasters do, while hiding away its pearls on channels that they know almost nobody watches, in what way will it be a public service system deserving our payment of a whacking great annual licence fee?

(Chris Dunkley, *Financial Times*, 21 June 2000)

In April 2000, the Director-General, Greg Dyke, said:

Audiences with digital television can already receive up to 200 channels. The BBC will have to fight hard to retain its share and reach in this transformed environment. Though the BBC is still the most-watched broadcaster in multi-channel homes, we will only retain this position if we really understand our audiences and can create programmes with the flair and distinctiveness that they expect from the BBC. We face a particularly tough challenge in winning young audiences, many of whom have been brought up in multi-channel homes.

(Greg Dyke, *Ariel*, April 2000)

Three months later, the man Mr Dyke appointed as Director of Television, Mark Thompson, indicated that the BBC was thinking of turning BBC 1 into an entertainment and news channel, and re-naming the existing digital channels BBC 3, 4 and 5. In this way, serious and minority appeal programmes would no longer find their way onto the mainstream, mass-audience channels. Clearly this would improve BBC 1's share of viewing, which has been falling. As BBC 1 takes more than a third of the licence fee (£832 million of £2,318 million), this would be a redefinition of public service broadcasting, which would allow people to question the principles underlying BBC funding. At present, BBC 1 includes 14 different types of programme, including religion, music and current affairs.

Mark Thompson spoke of Britain's cultural elite as 'just one more niche', not necessarily in touch with the wider public. One suspects he may regard religion in much the same way. He seemed to be hinting that the first changes based on a new philosophy could be implemented by the autumn of 2001 with a complete transition from the mixing of programme types on a given channel by 2005. The Secretary of State for Culture, Chris Smith, was reported in *The Guardian* on 19 June 2000 as having expressed surprise at these proposals and repeated his belief in the value of a mixed schedule for BBC 1.

Maggie Brown, in *The Guardian* on the same day, speculated that BBC policy could be to redefine public service broadcasting before the legislation promised in the next Parliament. Perhaps, she thought, the BBC saw room for change now, which could be prevented in the future by strict controls on content, channel by channel. It is worth noting that ITV and the ITC still appear committed to a mixed, diverse schedule.

Within a matter of days, Greg Dyke went on the record himself in *The Daily Telegraph*. He pointed out that *BBC News* at 9 p.m. on BBC 1 attracted only 10 per cent of the viewing audience in digital homes. But when asked whether the new policy would ghettoize serious programmes, he said: 'I doubt very much whether that will be the case. The idea that we're going to abandon all factual programming and news on BBC 1 isn't true. It's much more a case of shifting emphasis rather than a fundamental shift. The important question to me is: "What is your mix of programming overall and how much are you prepared to spend on it?"' To the list of 'appropriate' programmes for BBC 1 he added 'news and events'. 'By events, I'd include a lot of factual programmes – *Walking with Dinosaurs* is an event' (Greg Dyke, *The Daily Telegraph*, 22 June 2000).

The channels' broad designation would appear to be: BBC 1 to concentrate even more on entertainment, comedy, drama and the BBC's big budget programmes; BBC 2 to show serious documentaries, arts and new comedy; BBC Choice would be aimed at young people; BBC Knowledge would be the outlet for educational programmes, which are to receive substantial additional funding, whilst the new digital channel, BBC 5, would be devoted to high culture and the arts. According to Tom Leonard who interviewed the Director-General for *The Daily Telegraph*, he recognized that he would have to find a lot more money, £400–500 million, to ensure that he can provide distinctive programmes for as many as five television channels. *BBC News 24* and *BBC Parliament* were not mentioned.

He appeared dismissive of those who might disagree with such a policy for a public service broadcaster saying: 'The history of the BBC is littered with times when change had to be made and when those who liked what was already there were quite successful in making a big fuss about it' (Greg Dyke, *The Daily Telegraph*, 22 June 2000).

In the *Financial Times*, one of the most distinguished television critics, Chris Dunkley, said:

In the 21st century world of Tony Blair, the idea of setting an example, leading from the front, telling people what you believe in and challenging them to follow you is anathema. These days you don't tell people what your ideas are, you ask them. Focus groups or, failing that, raw ratings, will tell you what people want and you simply hand back large quantities of whatever they tell you ... Apply it to television and there is little doubt about what you will be told to supply: soap operas, sport and *Who Wants to be a Millionaire?*

(*Financial Times*, 21 June 2000)

He quoted a comment written after Mr Dyke had become the ratings saviour of TV-am by introducing the cartoon character, Roland Rat: 'The cartoon is an essential ingredient in this meticulously research cocktail of triviality. TV-am is trite, but not by accident. This is what the public wants – the figures prove it.'

Having included that in his article, Chris Dunkley concluded: 'The broad idea of dedicated channels is not necessarily a bad one, even if the scrapping of mixed-schedule networks is highly questionable ... What is so ominous for the future of the BBC is the tone, language and underlying attitude.' He quoted from Mark Thompson's speech:

The whole question of what is and what isn't valuable in broadcasting, or in the arts or in any aspect of culture, is itself up for debate ... The BBC has real responsibilities to audiences not interested in the cultural agenda of arts documentaries, classical music and so on. Sometimes proponents of high culture really do sound as though they believe we're talking about 'pearls before swine', the only irritation being that now the swine have somehow got hold of the remote control. We can't think like that.

(Chris Dunkley, quoting Mark Thompson, *Financial Times*, 21 June 2000)

What the future will hold, as audiences to the traditional mainstream channels fall, we cannot know. The BBC points out that in multi-channel homes in Wales, the audience for the *BBC News* at 6 p.m. and 9 p.m. has fallen by 40 per cent. Men and children, apparently, are using the electronic programme guide (EPG) which selects automatically the types of programme people say they like, rather than looking at the schedules published in newspapers and magazines.

Billed as the harbinger of 'personal television' EPGs can be used to select given types of programme the viewer enjoys but soon will be web-based allowing people to link to programme reviews, chat on-line and receive e-mails. The second new device is called TiVo, which is an 'intelligent' video recorder. It can store up to 30 hours of programmes on a hard disk and record one programme whilst another is being viewed. It can also effectively 'pause' live programmes if you are interrupted whilst you are watching, so allowing you to watch what remains later. The BBC is clearly concerned at the implications of these gadgets for the way in which people use television. However, if they make channels as such redundant, the question could be posed, why scrap BBC 1 and BBC 2 in their current mixed form?

For there is the risk, one suspects, of an even sharper fall in the viewing of serious programmes if they are no longer to be found in the mainstream analogue channels which will, probably for a decade yet, remain the only BBC television available to the many who do not acquire digital before the analogue service is finally switched off. At the very time that the BBC Religious Broadcasting Department is maintaining that its offerings could be more broadly based and therefore appealing to wider audiences than they do today, they could be placed out of the reach of many people who most value them and away from those who might chance upon something which could prove unexpectedly to be of help at a given point in life. Vigilance will be required in the coming years and the churches will need to become adept at presenting the case for public service principles to be retained in British broadcasting with skill and conviction.

To conclude on a more encouraging note, radio seems likely to be less affected by the impending changes of the digital age. The new Controller, Radio 4, Helen Boaden, made her first public speech since taking that job at the Churches' Broadcasting Conference at Swanwick on 13 June 2000. She spoke of the fact that 'religious broadcasting and the BBC have grown up together', with *Sunday Half-hour* on Radio 2 having just celebrated its 60th birthday and the *Daily Service* and *Choral Evensong* both having been broadcast for more than 70 years. She said 'that part of their power to move and engage audiences is due to their continuity. They connect us to a profound, shared tradition of Christian worship.'

She spoke of her own interview for the post at which she had emphasized the importance of religion to the Radio 4 listener, whose average age is 54. Her view was that 'the network has no qualms about scheduling a series with clear religious subject matter ... because it recognizes that people who are interested in ideas are also interested in ideas about religion'. She maintained that:

The BBC's commitment to formal religious broadcasting is clear. But we also try to engage audiences, who have no particular religious faith or commitment, in the deeper issues of existence, in the spiritual dimension of life. And the way we do that is not just through programmes labelled 'religious'. It's by threading difficult ethical and moral issues through mainstream programmes. To me it's very important that *Thought for the Day* is sitting in the middle of the *Today* programme at a prime time in the morning, demanding that just for a few minutes we move beyond the news agenda and reflect.

One of the most powerful pieces I ever heard about the nature of religious faith was not on a conventional religious programme at all. It was on *Home Truths* on a Saturday morning, when we heard the story of a woman who was attacked by a young man wielding a knife on her doorstep. It was terrifying. She very nearly died. But her retelling of that appalling experience and her simple explanation of how her religious faith helped her cope and forgive has stayed with me and, I am sure, many other listeners. That, for me, was an important exploration of religious experience aimed not at those who already know what they believe but at those who may not.

> (Helen Boaden, Churches' Broadcasting Conference,
> 13 June 2000)

Turning to television, Helen Boaden admitted the difficulties of predicting the digital future – 'the fourth revolution in broadcasting' – but felt there was a bright side,

because the new technology does create radical new possibilities for religious programmes … You might imagine, for example, a digital television channel that was a lot like Radio 4, where religion played an important role. No one's planning it yet but it's one of the possibilities being thrown up by the digital revolution, which poses exciting possibilities and huge challenges for all of us. No one at the BBC, and I am sure ITV, would pretend that anyone has all the answers. We are learning with everyone else, and like everyone else we are somewhat taken aback by the speed of technological change. What I would say, though, is that without its public service core, which includes religious broadcasting, the BBC would not be the BBC. And to that very important extent your fate and ours are inextricably linked over the coming 'interesting' years.

> (Helen Boaden, Churches' Broadcasting Conference,
> 13 June 2000)

Interesting years and a high risk policy for public service broadcasting were unveiled soon after Helen Boaden spoke. First came the announcement in the BBC staff newspaper *Ariel* on 11 July 2000 that 'the role of Head of Religion will be refocused… A new post, Head of Religion and Ethics, will work across the BBC to develop a cross-media editorial strategy,' below whom there will, in Manchester, be a 'creative director for religion'. As a former Head of BBC Religious Broadcasting, David Winter, wrote in the *Church Times* of 28 July 2000, this latter is 'a post for which God himself would seem to be the only suitably qualified candidate'. A letter he had received from the BBC claimed that these changes would 'place religion where it belongs – "at the heart of a creative powerhouse of the best documentary specialists"'.

Six weeks later the wider multi-channel future for BBC Television was unveiled by the Director-General, Greg Dyke, in the MacTaggart Lecture at the Edinburgh International Television Festival on 25 August. He claimed that public service broadcasting was 'the glue which binds this society together in the digital age' (*The Scotsman*, 26 August 2000). He proceeded to announce the move of the *Nine O'Clock News* to an hour later and then outlined the themes of the 'suite' of channels to be offered.

BBC 1 – Mainstream television – Universal, popular drama, comedy and documentaries, news and sport.
BBC 2 – Key leisure and lifestyle programmes, thoughtful analysis, creatively ambitious drama and comedy and specialist sport.

BBC 3 – Original British comedy, drama and music as well as arts, education and social action aimed at a young audience. Also, during the day, programmes for pre-school children.

BBC 4 – Unashamedly intellectual, a mixture of Radios 3 and 4 on television. It will be based around arts, challenging music, ideas and in-depth discussion. Daytime is for children, 6-13.

BBC News 24 – As already available in homes with digital receivers.

BBC Parliament – The proceedings broadcast in vision via digital satellite and cable but sound only on terrestrial digital transmission.

According to *The Guardian* on 28 August 2000, Greg Dyke admitted after his lecture 'that his proposition depended upon harnessing talent in a way never before achieved at the BBC'. The cost of ensuring that all five channels, plus the additional children's services are of high quality will be great and according to a former member of BBC staff, Steve Hewlett, who is now Director of Programmes at Carlton, 'There is a creative cultural problem within the BBC that goes deeper than lack of money' (*The Guardian*, 28 August 2000). Given that one-third of all BBC licence fee income is at present spent on BBC 1 alone and that in addition to these new television channels the BBC has to maintain five radio networks and 45 local radio stations and will give regional television in England £64 million, in Scotland £31 million, in Wales and Nortern Ireland £21 million each per annum, there must be a real concern as to whether there will be enough money to ensure high quality throughout. It is not overstating the risk to say that the future of the BBC, the licence fee, and the ethos of public service broadcasting both in radio and television will hinge on the way in which the BBC rises to the challenge the new Director-General has set.

If the BBC doesn't deliver real innovation and programmes that the commercial market doesn't deliver, the licence fee will not be renewed in seven years' time and neither will the Royal Charter. But if we spend that money well and please our audiences and surprise and delight and amaze them, then it will. And I think it will and that's a forecast – providing we do our stuff.

(Sir Christopher Bland, BBC Chairman, *The Times*,
23 June 2000)

Postscript

The Lord's Prayer

Finally, what might be described as 'The Lord's Prayer' for a new mood in Broadcasting House. The Birt years were dark indeed and for many most dispiriting, particularly for religious broadcasters. No Christian consideration of the BBC at this time should ignore the manner in which the Corporation has been managed in the 1990s. In the House of Lords, Baroness James of Holland Park (the author P.D. James), who was until recently herself a BBC Governor, articulated the worries most effectively:

Perhaps my greatest concern at the moment is the managerial ethos of the BBC. I see it as increasingly too rigidly controlled, too bureaucratic, too secretive and too arrogant. The product of the BBC is not a commodity; it is creativity in sound and vision. Creativity does not flourish in an atmosphere of despotism, coercion or fear. It is not nourished by the shibboleths of fashionable managerial theories, by the filling in of innumerable forms or by directives issued in that curious bureaucratic jargon which bears little relation to the English language. And at the heart of creativity we have not a system, but people, men and women, on whose dedication, loyalty and talents the Corporation depends. Systems exist to serve them. They do not exist to serve the system. I wish that the BBC today was a happier place in which creative people could work and flourish ... The BBC should stand for three things: integrity, independence, excellence. If it fails even in one of these it will lose the confidence of the country and will no longer retain or indeed deserve its long-standing reputation as the world's most trusted and admired public service broadcaster. I hope – indeed, in my more optimistic moments, I am confident – that it will not fail.

(*Hansard*, 3 March 1999)

The Bishop's Plea

We have not made our case strongly enough over the years – we did not fight our corner and I accept the guilt. How are we to safeguard the Gospel across the airwaves? We ought to give a lot more attention to that. We must recognise that there is a very cold world coming up for religious broadcasting and proclaiming Good News. If we do not attend to our communication needs, the Good News we've been involved in proclaiming for 2000 years will become silenced in future broadcasting. We have the major task to keep the rumour of God alive.

(The late Bill Westwood, then Bishop of Peterborough, General Synod, 1989)

The Producer's Purpose

We should show all religious activities that are taking place and all other activities to which religion is directly relevant. We should show all forms of religious teaching, raise necessary questions, and strive in every way to show that Christianity is a vital and life-enhancing religion concerned with the needs of today. We should do all this – but no more. It is not for us to compel or to indoctrinate our audience. It is for those who watch our efforts to accept or reject – but at least, we hope, to consider – what we, in all humility, present.

(*About Religion*, Michael Redington (ed.), 1963)

Appendix A
What the Papers Say

The Daily Telegraph – 15 February 2000

It is rare for great British institutions to fall out, but the General Synod of the Church of England is girding up its loins to chastise the BBC ... Although it is late in the day for the Church to take on the Corporation, the battle is not yet lost ... There are excellent religious documentaries – all too often, though, religious programmes deliberately subvert religion in general and Christianity in particular. An aggressively critical secularism animates much coverage; the underlying assumption being that religion is a primitive anthropological phenomenon, fit to be ridiculed but not to be taken seriously. Yet there is no reason why religion should be singled out in this way. Programmes on gardening or sport work on the assumption that their viewers enjoy and approve of these activities. Religion, too, should be seen as a practical activity. The BBC should take a leaf out of the success of cookery and other 'how to' programmes. Most viewers need spiritual no less than edible nourishment, and just as many would like to be told how to pray as enjoy being shown how to boil an egg. The potential for a new Delia of the God slot ought to make even Greg Dyke's BBC relish synergy with the Synod. – *Leader*

The Guardian – 7 January 2000

Few people realise just how inconsistent was BBC policy throughout the Birt years. The Himalayan heights (of programme aspiration) gave way to the pressure for ratings, which has given way again. – *Media*

The Tablet – 6 November 1999

Inspired by a report from the Churches' Advisory Council for Local Broadcasting called *Losing Faith in the BBC*, *Sunday* (Radio 4, 24 October), one of the last bastions of religious broadcasting, sent Martin Stott to investigate … This was a brave, hard-hitting report, to which senior BBC Production executives declined to contribute … It is a pity that the *Sunday* programme has been pushed to such an early time-slot that many would still be abed. – *Margaret Howard, Radio Critic*

The Daily Telegraph – 22 February 2000

Radio 4's nightly arts magazine, *Front Row*, had a go at discussing whether the BBC is marginalising religious broadcasting. I won't have been the only person talking back to the radio, asking whether there can be any doubt. Not only is there less than there was a decade ago, what there is comes either disguised as a star vehicle or gets transmitted at distinctly off-peak times. – *Gillian Reynolds, Radio Critic*

The Tablet – 4 March 2000

Religion is one of a dozen or so subjects that now rarely crop up in prime time, from classical music to drama, architecture to serious politics. But religious programmes themselves are often pitched at the lowest common denominator and Ernie Rea [Head of BBC Religious Broadcasting] defends this policy. – *Leader*

The Tablet – 13 November 1999

The BBC department which deals with religious programmes may change its name. Mr Rea said it could be argued that the word 'religion' had become a hindrance, since it 'artificially narrows the BBC's vision of what religious broadcasting could and should be'. Mr Rea argued that while traditional Christianity was in decline in the United Kingdom with 'a chronic absence of young people' attending Protestant churches and Catholicism 'in crisis', a new kind of spirituality was growing. That phenomenon, along with other faiths such as Islam and Hinduism, should be better represented in the BBC's religious coverage – hence the change of name. To members of minority faiths he declared: 'This is your BBC too.'

Ariel – 2 November 1999

Religion 'should not be confined to one department', but the BBC's Manchester-based Religious Broadcasting Department is a 'powerhouse of creativity' producing radio programmes such as Radio 4's *The Moral Maze* and Radio 3's *The Brains Trust*. – *Jenny Abramsky, Director, Radio*

Ariel – 9 November 1999

The BBC plans to use the internet to strengthen its religious output. In a few months they [*The Daily Service*] will use the internet to enable those who are currently united by listening to join an electronic spiritual community. The BBC is also considering putting permanent microphones into centres of worship. This could result in BBC Online computers connecting to the central mosque in Manchester each Friday in order to 'pipe the prayers to the world'.

The Daily Telegraph – 17 February 2000

Joan Bakewell, who has presented the moral affairs discussion programme *Heart of the Matter* for twelve years, said she felt the BBC's religious output had been neglected. Her final series of the programme returns this Sunday at 11.35 p.m., by which time many potential viewers are likely to have gone to bed … 'Religion has had year-on-year budget cuts and has been moved later and later at night', she said. 'When you've experienced that for ten years you begin to wonder whether anyone's got much trust in you. All of us sigh when we learn where we've been scheduled.' Peter Salmon, Controller, BBC 1 said, 'I'm very grateful to Joan for the work she's done but she doesn't know the full picture about what's happening to religion on BBC 1 and about our plans for new output and new programmes. Times have changed and we need to reflect that and look at things differently.'

The Independent – 18 February 2000

The last I heard, 'looking at things differently' included scrapping the 'religious affairs' tag altogether and renaming it 'faith and values'. Very now, very Totnes, very awkward and embarrassed about conventional religious values, very suggestive of cringingly patronising trendy vicars trying to be hip. And indeed the trendy vicar who is Head of BBC Religious Broadcasting, Ernie Rea, defends his record saying, 'the BBC has become more audience focussed' … I'm not religious myself, so I'm not irritated by the BBC's craven attitude towards religious broadcasting for personal reasons. It's not that I feel neglected. It's that surely a public service broadcaster should be tackling religious issues without being too 'audience focussed'. – *Deborah Orr*

The Times – 26 February 2000

The Big End was a good effort, a fair attempt, but it was flawed. I'm slightly disappointed that the churches should castigate us for making the effort, but there has been a change in the relationship between the BBC and the Church of England; [it] has become more tense and testing. – *Ernie Rea*

Church Times – 12 May 2000

I suppose there is a place for such a programme [*Heaven and Earth Show*], aimed at the populace uncontaminated by the virus of faith but happy enough to be prodded every now and again towards the margins of that foreign land, religious belief and practice: but for this to be our public service network's only Sunday morning programme containing any trace of religion is little short of a national disgrace. – *Gillean Craig, television critic*

Christian Herald – 6 November 1999

Come off it, Beeb – If it was a theological concept that made any sense, Lord Reith would be turning in his grave. The lecture given by the BBC's Head of Religious Broadcasting shows exactly the extent to which the BBC has 'dumbed down' … With talk of 'The New Religious' – those people of 'vague faith' – as the new target audience, Rea turns his back finally on the practice of public service broadcasting with strong Christian roots. He's right to say the media is out of step with the new spiritual climate in the UK. But if the likes of *The Heaven and Earth Show* is the answer, heaven help us … The truth is: the powers-that-be don't think authentic Christianity makes good TV. – *Leader*

The Tablet – 13 November 1999

As the BBC's Head of Religious Broadcasting, he has to defend publicly that which he may feel privately to be indefensible. – *Roger Bolton*

Methodist Recorder – 2 March 2000

The downgrading of religion by the BBC evoked a resolution at last year's Methodist Conference, which led to interesting meetings but no action … This process of downgrading is denied by the Reverend Ernie Rea. He has to say that, of course, or he would find himself back in parish ministry quicker than you can say *Songs of Praise*, but the fact is, as everyone knows who has eyes, ears and a clock, that religion has been pushed to the very margins with reduced staff and budgets. – *David Bridge*

Church Times – 25 February 2000

BBC religious programme-makers work wearing a double ball and chain, one ball marked Birt and the other marked Manchester. [The Religious Department based in Manchester] should be replaced by a commissioning editor and a small team of executive producers with a budget they can use to buy in material from independent producers. The Department in Manchester now has no money available to invest speculatively in anything that has not previously been taken through the complicated internal commissioning system. – *Ted Harrison*

The Independent – 4 March 2000

The Controller, BBC 1, Peter Salmon, has been scheduling them [*Everyman* and *Heart of the Matter*] later and later, thus reducing the audience and creating the impression that there is no demand for them. To communicate with [the people of vague faith] both religious leaders and broadcasters need to explore the uncharted ground where contemporary sensibilities encounter the old questions about how the hunger for spirituality connects with the concerns for day-to-day life. But they must do so in a way which is non-judgemental, non-simplistic, non-dogmatic, non-dismissive and non-cynical.

The Independent – 23 December 1999

Ernie Rea … has two 'major landmark series' in the pipeline … The first is *Son of God,* a three-part series in which 'an agnostic BBC personality' will go to Israel and 'recreate the greatest story ever told' by swimming in the Sea of Galilee, spending a night in the wilderness, going to Jerusalem at Passover and so on … The second is a 'spiritual audit of the nation'. This twelve-part series will 'take the temperature' of the various faith communities across the UK. – *Clare Garner*

The Daily Express – 21 February 2000

Emma Freud's BBC series will cover religion and sex. 'Ultimately we can't decide when and how sex is right or wrong,' said Freud. 'In the confusion, religion has become a powerful moral influence.' The Head of Religious Broadcasting, Ernie Rea, insisted, 'We are absolutely committed to high quality religious programmes which will make an impact.'

The Guardian – 24 February 2000

Pressed to offer more programming, the Religious Affairs Department has now come up with such highlights as Emma Freud on religion and sex and a series called *Soul of Britain* investigating the country's 'spiritual free market'.

The Sunday Times – 20 February 2000

As interest in feng shui supersedes flower arranging, the BBC is joining converts to the 'new religion'. Ernie Rea said, 'The new religious have a belief and we should reflect it. They buy huge numbers of books on these subjects like *Men are from Mars, Women are from Venus*. They are not nutters.' Joan Bakewell said, 'BBC Religion should not be taking things like feng shui seriously. Feng shui is lifestyle, it is not religion and not even faith. It's as if *Top Gear* decided to start looking at bicycles, not cars.'

The Church of England Newspaper – 25 February 2000

To those who have no religious grounding, to be told about feng shui one week and star gazing the next is likely to leave them seeing religion as gobbledy-gook, belonging in the pages of one of Roald Dahl's mystical, magical books. – *Jonathan Wynne-Jones*

The Daily Telegraph – 1 March 2000

The Church of England is to join with organisations such as the Mothers' Union to set up an independent watchdog to monitor the quality of religious programmes on television. The decision by the General Synod follows growing concern … With the support of several bishops, the watchdog will maintain a year-round vigil … Nigel Holmes, a retired BBC producer, called some populist BBC religious programmes such as *The Big End*, 'trite drivel'.

The Guardian – 1 March 2000

A BBC spokeswoman said: 'The Corporation welcomes the very constructive and intelligent debate at Synod, although we remain concerned that some criticisms about our religious output are founded on flawed statistics.'

The Scotsman – 15 February 2000

We in the Church of Scotland certainly get far better religious coverage than they do in England. – *Alison Elliot, Convenor, Church and Nation Committee*

Broadcast – 3 March 2000

Channel 4 Commissioning Editor, History, Arts and Religion, Janice Hadlow feels that the key to boosting the quality of the [religious] genre is attracting the best people to make the programmes. 'We are beginning to see a real ability to attract the top film-makers and putting these programmes out in prime time is tremendously important.'

Broadcast – 3 March 2000

Religion – It could become the new rock 'n' roll. No, really. As with business and science programming, broadcasters are now crying out for interesting new formats to attract new audiences … Nearly all insist that the genre should not be a burden on their schedules, consigned to a ratings wasteland and viewed only by card-carrying Christians. – *Ashley Davies*

Christian Herald – 18 March 2000

My hope is that in view of the considerable public concern over recent weeks, Mr Dyke will take a long, hard look at how this public service is really meeting the spiritual needs of the British public … The Christian community is one of the most significant and caring groups in our nation, yet we are pilloried and poked fun at year in, year out … The meaning of life is something which should be 'prime time' for every person alive. – *Rob Frost, Methodist Evangelist*

The Church of England Newspaper – 31 March 2000

Joel Edwards, General Director, Evangelical Alliance, struck out at the media's lack of church coverage ... He said that he felt that the uphill struggle to make the church credible had become even steeper in the three years since he became General Director. Mr. Edwards' grievances are a further indication of the 'glorious indifference' of the media towards the church ... The media's cynicism does nothing to diminish our relevance.

The Sunday Telegraph – 16 April 2000

The creators of a new BBC drama series for Easter starring Helen Baxendale, Jonathan Price and Joss Acland, have accused executives of broadcasting it late at night because it deals with religion ... In addition to an all-star cast, the series has attracted some leading writers, including the veteran playwright Arnold Wesker ... BBC executives changed its name to make it more obviously religious and then scheduled the monologues for the 'graveyard slot' with most appearing just before midnight. The Bishop of Liverpool said that the BBC remained deaf to the vast audience who wanted good religious programmes in the mainstream of broadcasting. Norman Stone, who produced the series, said that it had suffered from 'an ancient knee-jerk reaction that religion must be put on late because it won't attract an audience'. Mr Stone created the award-winning *Shadowlands* about C.S. Lewis. Ernie Rea said, 'It was felt that because these dramas are considered, thoughtful pieces, they suit the later evening slots when the audience has time to sit and enjoy them.'

Private Eye – 25 February 2000

BBC Attacks Church of England

By Our Religious Staff – Sir Clifford Longley-Richard

The Church of England is accused of sidelining religion in a shock report compiled for the BBC. Sir Greg Dyke accuses the church of 'trivialising important issues' and 'dumbing down the content of services'.

Carey in the Community – 'All they do is talk about sex and gays. There's no attempt to deal with the real issues of religion at all.' An angry Archbishop of Canterbury hit back saying, 'We have to appeal to all sections of the community and in particular to young people. If this means changing our methods of presentation and placing more emphasis on pop music, then so be it.'

How to Make a Bakewell Tart – 1. Put her programme on very late at night. 2. Leave there for twelve years until Bakewell boils over. 3. Remove from television and allow to simmer gently.

BBC staff newspaper, Ariel – 11 July 2000

Manchester will retain its religious specialism whilst developing a broader documentary portfolio. The Head of Religion role will be refocused. Reporting to the directors of the BBC Factual and Learning Programme Department, this new position – Head of Religion and Ethics – will work across the BBC to develop a cross-media editorial strategy. In addition, a creative director for Religion will be appointed in Manchester.

Appendix B

Summary of the Debate in the
General Synod of the Church of England
29 February 2000

BBC Religious Broadcasting
Amended motion passed by 370 / 0

That this Synod:

e) express its gratitude to broadcasters who have, over the years, accurately reflected and vastly enriched the spiritual life of the nation with coherent, intelligent, entertaining and engaging religious broadcasts;

f) regret the reduction and rescheduling of certain religious broadcasts by the BBC and call on the Corporation, in the context of their public service commitments and statutory responsibilities to a changing society, to maintain and develop high quality religious programmes, including worship especially for the housebound, for present and future analogue and digital channels which are made to high production values, designed for a general audience, including young people, and carried at peak listening and viewing times;

g) call on the churches to support and engage with those involved in broadcasting in creative and imaginative ways, helping our culture to explore faith not as an additional element to an otherwise secular world but as a part of it;

h) ask the Archbishops' Council to develop, in co-
    operation with other churches and interested parties,
    a mechanism for monitoring and reporting on the
    provision and quality of religious output by the BBC
    and the commercial sector.

Nigel Holmes (Diocese of Carlisle) moved the motion:

Synod speechmakers are fond of saying that they love the
Church of England before proceeding to launch a savage
attack on the object of their affections. I love the BBC and
the principles of public service broadcasting and indeed I
was proud to work for the Corporation for many years. So
what I say is said in love and the words are those of a
devotee.

The relationship of Church to Corporation was close
from the founding by John Reith. He saw to it that the first
advisory council was that for religion – today's Central
Religious Advisory Committee. Mr Reith lived between
here and Smith Square, at 6 Barton Street, and one day in
March 1923 this young man, only 33, invited the Archbishop of Canterbury to dinner. In his autobiography he
says that to his Anglican wife the Archbishop was not far
removed from the Deity. Randall Davidson was that Archbishop and at the dinner party Mrs Davidson asked John
Reith the memorable question: 'Do we need to open the
windows for the wireless to receive?' As the valves began
to glow and the music play, so the Archbishop's heart was
slowly warmed by the allure of this new medium. So for
half a century and more, a really rather cosy relationship
continued between this country's oldest and youngest
national institutions.

Three-quarters of a century on, I had a hunch that much
had, imperceptibly, been lost from BBC Religious Broadcasting within the span of just a few years. As a member of

the Churches' Advisory Council for Local Broadcasting, I was encouraged to do some digging. What came up was more disturbing than I had imagined – total output on BBC 1 and 2 up by a half over ten years, yet religious output down by a third. BBC network religious radio hours had fallen by an unprecedented 15 per cent in a single year (1998/99), the last for which figures were available.

The Radio 4 changes of April 1998 had caused a significant loss of audience to the flagship *Sunday* programme, and those religious Sunday evening television programmes which remained were screened ever later. In one case that was no bad thing. The series at this time last year, *The Big End*, I described to the London *Evening Standard* a couple of weeks ago as 'trite drivel'. I stand by that description for the particular series, but as the national dailies ran with the story after that, I was disturbed to see it applied more generally. I would like to say at this point that I have nothing but admiration for the staff of BBC Religious Broadcasting who work week in, week out, with ever fewer resources to make many splendid and uplifting programmes.

Whilst the praise is flowing, could I say a word in support of BBC Local Radio, where the resources are even fewer but the two hours or more of religious output a week often strong and supported in some cases by the secondment of staff from the churches? ITV too draws strength from its church advisers, one of whom, the Bishop of Ludlow, wrote to me about Carlton in the Midlands where 'there is a real commitment to religious broadcasting as an important part of the schedule'. ITV has shown in recent weeks that such programmes can be audience winners – programmes like *Bethlehem Year Zero*, which with transmission times ranging from 10.45 p.m. to 12.15 a.m. over six nights managed to draw an audience well in excess of four million, greatly beyond the expectations of the schedulers. This month ITV ran a series featuring young people investigating the parables and speaking to world figures of faith. It's called *What's it All About?*

I can today reveal for the first time some most recent facts and figures. BBC 1 produced 42 hours of religious programmes in the first six months of the current financial and programme year. In the same period the ITV network alone carried 49, almost 20 per cent more than the licence-fee funded BBC, and of course as the Bishop of Ludlow mentioned, most ITV stations transmit considerably more when you include their locally-produced religious programmes. I have also discovered that the *Everyman/ Heart of the Matter* slot has been filled for 20 weeks this financial year. Only a few years ago they ran for 48 weeks. This presumably is as a result of £250,000 being taken just before that year started from the budget of the religious broadcasting department in Manchester to fund digital channels, which are virtually devoid of religious or spiritual content.

Now is the time to persuade the BBC to write 'public service broadcasting' in larger letters. With a new Director-General and soon a new Controller, Radio 4, and with the forthcoming licence fee increase, the time could not be better. They cannot but be chastened by Joan Bakewell's accusations of continual budget cuts year after year, ever later transmission times and overall 'neglect' – her word, not mine. Melvyn Bragg, a fellow Cumbrian, has written to me about what he regards as the sorry state of religious broadcasting and many missed opportunities. A former Head of BBC Religious Broadcasting also wrote to me to say that Synod would be well advised to take this motion very seriously indeed. I am most grateful to the record number of members whose signatures have prompted this debate.

Bernadette Burbridge (Diocese of York):

If broadcasting is effective, it is able to act as a mirror to our society, according to Colin Morris, a former Head of BBC Religious Broadcasting. It reflects the quality of our culture and helps to clarify our priorities. If the mirror is true, we may see not only what we are but what we may become. We can ask ourselves if our priorities are the right ones and whether or not they will actually bring us the desires of our hearts. Now a mirror will also show us what we do not want to see. If there is a dumbing-down element to our culture, we will see that. If our priorities are health and wealth, we will see that. Our question is if our priorities are mission and evangelization, will broadcasters show us that too? I think the answer is yes and no. What we understand as mission and evangelization is about the simple day-to-day life of the church, about being the presence of church in our community – it is about Christ alive in us. It doesn't make good programmes. It's about how we ought to be.

My challenge to the BBC is that more could be done and it's something we haven't seen for a long time. Faith is about story, about imagination, about opening oneself to the possibility of change and of hope through encounter with God. In a broadcasting climate where news is god, most of what we receive as religious broadcasting is reporting. We get lovely stories told to us very well, but what we don't get is imaginative exploration of story and I would like our religious broadcasters to stop relying so much on the old and obvious religious forms of programmes. There is a great call for them to be made to live forever, but there are new opportunities. We need to be led to think more imaginatively about our faith through art, through television and radio drama, which gives us a chance to encounter the real questions of life imaginatively without being told all the time how somebody else did it or how they got through it. Truly those stories are inspirational but we also need to be allowed to engage our imaginations in possibility.

David Hope (Archbishop of York):

For two years I have been Chairman of the Central Religious Advisory Committee. I am entirely at ease with the suggestion Mr Holmes makes in his background paper that 'the future function of CRAC should be assessed'. Indeed, since becoming Chairman that is something I have been seeking to do and hopefully to some effect. However, I am mindful that the Committee does work within formal terms of reference which make it very clear that it is an advisory body – 'CRAC's opinion may be sought on the understanding that it has no powers to tell the broadcasting bodies what they may or may not do.'

However, 'CRAC may choose to act as a pressure group, bringing its influence to bear on the appropriate authorities' … One of the terms of reference states that it should be a bridge of communication between the broadcasting bodies and the religious constituency. There are, I believe, a number of ways in line with Mr Holmes's thinking, in which this could be further developed. One very positive move could be that the relationship between CRAC and the BBC Governors might become more in line with the relationship we have with the ITC where CRAC prepares an annual report and that report is presented to the Chairman personally, or a representative appointed by him, to the ITC … I am informed that a representative of the Governors is to be present at the next meeting of CRAC. I welcome this.

Robert Ellis (Diocese of Lichfield):

I'm glad that BBC Local Radio can be a source of pride both to us and to the BBC. BBC Radio Shropshire is the service to which most people in the county listen. Twenty years ago the Diocese of Lichfield decided to fund religious programmes on Local Radio. Now we spend £50,000 a year on two full-time producers, one at Stoke and the other at Shropshire. As a result the level and calibre of religious broadcasting on these two stations is superb. The broadcast worship at 9 a.m. on Radio Stoke attracts 60,000 listeners, that on Radio Shropshire which began just eighteen months ago, 20,000 at 7 a.m.

Jayne Ozanne (Archbishops' Council):

During my time at the BBC as part of the Senior Management Team for Broadcasting and Presentation, I was able to witness how the 'inner sanctum' of BBC Television is managed ... I helped write the channel marketing plans ... Not, I am sad to admit, in any of this work did I ever focus on religious broadcasting. Do you want to know why? The answer is in one little word, 'genre'. A 'genre' is a group of programmes, which all have the same style – drama, entertainment, daytime, sport, news, music, etc. It is these genres that become the focus of all BBC planning ... But you see religious broadcasting is not classed as a genre ... no central objectives are set for it and therefore there is no end of year measure and thus no central accountability. Until this changes there will, I predict, be little noticeable change to religious broadcasting within the BBC.

Nigel McCulloch (Bishop of Wakefield) who moved an amendment:

It's vital for this Synod to send an unmistakable message of regret at what has been happening to the content, scheduling and duration of some religious programmes. When these programmes are pushed to the margins of the schedules they become less accessible to audiences, thereby diminishing their status and endangering their quality. It's a downward spiral ... It's equally vital that we communicate to the BBC that quality religious broadcasting has its place in the schedules on merit and that, as Nigel Holmes has demonstrated, it can win the audiences broadcasters want ... I warn against religion being sidelined into the pay-ghetto existence of dedicated religious channels ... As the Annan Report put it: 'Religious questions often come up in moral and political terms and public service broadcasting has a role to help to discover a vocabulary and perhaps an iconography in which to meet them.'

A mechanism for monitoring the provision and quality of religious programmes in the future would send out a signal to all broadcasters that we are taking this matter very seriously and systematically. This is not to diminish the significance of CRAC, but that body is part of the broadcasters' own mechanism. My amendment asks the Archbishops' Council to develop this mechanism independently from the BBC and commercial sectors. Such a monitoring body, with co-operation from other churches and interested bodies, knowing who is broadcasting what and when, would lead to regular tabled qualitative as well as quantitative assessments. These would offer a 'health-check' on religious broadcasting, which I believe we need, and inform in an intelligent way general public debate.

Christina Rees (Diocese of St. Albans):

A society gets the media it deserves. What can we, as a church, do about the way our faith is portrayed? How will people listen to what we believe is the most important message of all if they can't understand us or if we stay in the equivalent of our upper rooms and praise God in unknown tongues in front of those who already believe? It is up to us to bridge the gap of understanding and convey what we believe in the media. If we do not like the image of what we see portrayed as Christianity, or if programmes are full of inaccuracies or misunderstandings, it is up to us to do something about it. Looking ahead, what are we doing to find the broadcasters, programme-makers, editors and controllers of the future? These people exist, but need the support, encouragement and opportunity if they are ever to test their calling.

Hugh Davidson (Church of Scotland observer):

All of us on the ecumenical bench share the conviction of the importance of religious broadcasting. In Scotland, the churches are more generously served by the BBC than is the case in England. We recognise that while the quantity of religious broadcasting is important and the timing of it is important too, the content is of no lesser importance. The churches will want to do what they can to ensure that discussions are balanced and that their position is recognisably presented. The Church of Scotland is very happy to be involved with the proposal to monitor programme output.

James Jones (Bishop of Liverpool):

The BBC is one of the major cultural institutions but the church must understand the BBC's boundaries. The purpose of religious broadcasting is to explore and reflect creatively and imaginatively the spiritual and moral aspects of life. But in an increasingly diverse and competitive media market, the broadcasters are more and more concerned about audiences and ratings. There is a recognised market for religious programmes. I say to those people concerned about market share, religious broadcasting is not minority broadcasting. It deals with faith and moral issues of interest to a wide general public. It is, and it ought to be, majority broadcasting for it deals with issues the majority of people are interested in. But not only is there a market for these programmes, there is also talent amongst the religious producers both in the BBC and in the independent sector. This talent and this market deserves investment in better budgets and much better scheduling. After my Holy Week series, *Word on the Street* (BBC 1 – 1999), the constant theme of letters I received was for earlier scheduling. This debate is not about special pleading on behalf of the churches. It is an encouragement and a challenge to the BBC to recognise that there is indeed a popular audience for well-budgeted and well-scheduled programmes.

David Webster (Diocese of Rochester) who moved an amendment:

I remember having lunch with Lord Reith. Then I was a young financial journalist. He had by then left the BBC and was chairman of British Oxygen … He was soon pointing out the errors of the BBC. That was forty years ago. My amendment refers to the housebound. I find, visiting those in nursing homes and alone in their own homes, elderly people who are bewildered, marginalized and indeed angered by the changes in timing, pattern and context of BBC Religious Broadcasting. They feel that their views are not being heard. Many find their radios cannot receive long wave, necessary for the *Daily Service*. Those in homes are unable to listen to Sunday morning worship at 8.10 a.m., as it clashes with breakfast. The BBC maintains that is a better time for churchgoers, so missing the main reason of broadcast worship which is for those who can't or won't be in church. The earlier *Songs of Praise* also clashes with Sunday supper!

Elaine Storkey (Diocese of London):

Humanism is dying. It's all but gone except, I must say, in the BBC. It's still rampant there in a whole range of ways, as is Christianity. But our culture as a whole is still deeply religious. It's got a very spiritual thread going through it. It's also full of pluralism, diversity, cynicism and in a sense the world view that we now have is distrusting, rejecting, incredulous towards big explanations, wacky, eclectic and so on. This is the context of our contemporary culture. 'Everything is relative.' And, of course, relativism can't itself be stated. What about the statement, 'Everything is relative'? Is that statement relative or absolute? It no longer matters whether we can state a position or not. It's something people hold amorphously. Christianity too is changing. It reflects more of the pluralism, the diversity, the experimentation, the youthfulness, the creativity of the culture.

Last week a BBC programmer 'phoned me up and asked me to be on a programme. It wasn't a religious programme. She commented on the fact that I was broadcasting on religion. She said, 'I don't know why they bother with that these days, it's so irrelevant.' I asked, 'What's your position, then?' She said, 'I don't have a position, I just don't believe God exists.' So I replied, 'Well, that's your position and that will colour everything you do and shape, your broadcasting and everything.' And she thought about it for a moment and said, 'Well, I'm just normal.' I said, 'No, you just reinvented normality to exclude God.' If we have broadcasters and programmers who actually believe a God exists, a God of love, it will be a very different programme … the results will be different. Let's pray for our broadcasters, that they will have the courage of their convictions and produce Christian world-view programmes.

Appendix C

A Chronicle of Christian Broadcast Coverage
Extracts from BBC Handbooks, Annual Reports and the Radio Times

1928 – The Service in the Pub

Dear Sir, – A patient of mine who keeps a small public house and a 'loud speaker' in the bar of the same, told me that what her clients liked best of all was the Church Service on Sunday evenings. Many of them came on purpose to hear it, and if the apparatus was out of order on any Sunday evening they grumbled exceedingly. No one was allowed to join in the hymns, but had to be prevented because singing is not allowed by the police on Sundays. I asked why, if they were so fond of church, they didn't go there, and she said it was a matter of pipes and glasses.

The next day I enquired at a very respectably-kept inn about a mile out in the country, where they also have a 'loud speaker'. The landlady told me the same story in almost the same words. But she gave a different explanation. She said that the service at their local church was dull and poor, whereas the Wireless 'Service' was very good with a good preacher, and she herself looked forward to it, and was very sorry if anyone wanted a drink, which she had to get up and serve during the 'service'.

(A West Country Doctor, letter to the *Radio Times* –
13 January 1928)

1936 – No development has been more marked than the gradual disappearance of the obviously nervous suspicion with which they (church leaders) first regarded the intrusion of 'wireless religion' and the growth, stage by stage, of their confidence and desire to co-operate. Two hundred and seventy ministers of religion broadcast during 1935. In that year the Sunday morning service was fixed at 9.30 a.m. 6.24 per cent of airtime was devoted to religion.

1945 – The Schools' Service was heard by 900,000 children each week. Of 23 religious broadcasts in the Home Programme, 20 are on weekdays. Increasingly, Religious Broadcasting seeks to do what the churches cannot do, and in this way the work adds to the impact of religion on society. There was a successful series of services for youth clubs.

1952 – Epilogues began on television and the Light Programme introduced a new daily programme consisting of a story, a hymn and a prayer.

1954 – Three per cent of national radio airtime was religious, as was eight per cent of regional output. One-third of the adult population heard at least one of the religious broadcasts on a Sunday. The primary aim of most religious broadcasting was evangelistic, to communicate the Christian Gospel effectively to those who are not active members of any local church.

1956 – *Jesus of Nazareth* was broadcast on children's television over eight weeks, culminating on Easter Day. *Meeting Point* began on television on Sundays from 7.00 – 7.25 p.m. It was planned mainly for viewers who are not members of any church.

1961 – *Songs of Praise* began with hymns introduced by a presenter, but without interviews.

1965 – Religious Broadcasting made a substantial contribution to BBC 2 within the pattern of programmes now being established. *Doubts and Certainties* included a memorable conversation between Billy Graham and David Frost. BBC 2 also carried a series of lectures on *The New Testament Gospels*. In radio, a series of programmes on the authority of the Bible marked a fresh approach to the educational aspects of Religious Broadcasting. As many people listened to *The People's Service* as went to church and even more watched *Songs of Praise*.

1971 – *Speakeasy* on Radio 1 with Jimmy Savile covered religious, ethical and social topics.

1974 – *The Sunday Debate* (chaired by Robin Day) and *Anno Domini* were launched at 6.15 p.m. on BBC 1. *Thank God It's Sunday* (an evening series) began on BBC 2. *In the Beginning* (on BBC 1) described the life of Jesus for children and was generally considered a great success.

1975 – *See You Sunday* reflected the religious world of the new generation. BBC 2 featured *Religious America*. Radio 3 carried a series on the Atonement, the Trinity and the Incarnation. The range of religious programmes on radio was greater now than it had ever been and showed no sign of lessening.

1977 – In consultation with the Central Religious Advisory Committee, the 'closed period' was reduced from 70 minutes (6.15–7.25 p.m.) to 35 minutes (6.40–7.15p.m.). The 70 minutes had been established in the 1950s. *Everyman* was to be broadcast no later than 10.15 p.m. on BBC 1.

1978 – *The Sunday Gang*, a morning children's programme began on BBC 1. It presented serious religious material in an imaginative and often light-hearted manner. Two short runs proved its capacity to draw a young audience. *Songs of Praise* was re-launched with interviews.

1980 – Gerald Priestland's *Today in Synod* was widely heard. In *Talkback* on Radio 1, young people discussed a serious spiritual issue. BBC 1 introduced *This is the Day* – worship from a viewer's house in place of a morning outside broadcast from a church.

1981 – *Wake up Sunday* (Children's BBC 1) proved very popular indeed. On Radio 2, *The People's Service* at 11.30 a.m. became *On the Way* and its audience doubled for a short time before religion was removed and the audience at that time fell. On Radio 4, *The Epilogue* ended.

1982 – The majority of viewers and listeners who had no religious commitment expected their media religion to be strong, simple and clearly defined. Over the past year there was undoubtedly a quickening of interest. Very few religious programmes were audience losers and some improved the ratings. The audience seemed particularly to like any illumination of authentic religious experience (testimony, in old terms) and help to relate faith and belief to everyday life. *Priestland's Progress* attracted 23,000 letters. BBC 1 Sunday worship was moved from noon to 9.30 a.m.

1984 – The *Morning Service* on Radio 4 achieved its largest regular audience for ten years. BBC 2 featured the Billy Graham evangelistic rallies. *Heart of the Matter* moved to Thursdays. *The Rock Gospel Show* – 'rock 'n' roll with an evangelical message' – BBC 1 Sundays at 5.15 p.m.

1986 – Listeners were concerned that the *Daily Service* was no longer available on a Saturday morning, even though an Evening Service had been introduced in its stead. *Lent '86*, a study course organized by the British Council of Churches, was accompanied by weekly programmes on Radio 4 culminating in an 80-minute documentary, *What on Earth is the Church For?*

1987 – The television drama, *Shadowlands*, broadcast in peak time won a BAFTA award as the best single drama of the year. 'We measure ourselves [Religious Broadcasting] against the very best of any area of radio and television output.' Apart from 6.40 to 7.15 p.m. on Sunday evenings, religious programmes took their chances in the mainstream. For three weeks in Lent the peak-time *Tuesday Call* on Radio 4 took Christian themes from the previous Sunday's *Morning Service* with the preacher in the studio to answer listeners' questions by telephone. *Umbrella*, 'a multi-faith story-telling programme for children' was launched.

1988 – *Five to Eleven* broadcast a reflection (thought) virtually every weekday of the year on BBC 1. At Easter, Radio 1 commissioned a tribute to Martin Luther King and at Christmas carried a gospel concert from a youth remand centre.

1989 – Brian Redhead presented the 13-part series *The Christian Centuries*. Radio 1 introduced an ethical panel game. *Everyman* and *Heart of the Matter* were seen throughout the year.

1991 – *Thought for the Day* celebrated its 30th anniversary – a survey showed that it was more popular than business, sport and parliamentary reports within the *Today* programme. *The Reith Lectures* on *The Persistence of Faith* were given by the Chief Rabbi-elect.

1992 – The Central Religious Advisory Committee held
a special meeting to discuss the transfer of Religious Broadcasting to Manchester. Members
feared that it would lead to the marginalization
of religion; that programme-makers, who would
have to work away from the national headquar-
ters of many religious organizations, would be
seriously hindered; that contact with senior
management would be reduced; and that a
number of experienced staff might leave rather
than remain with the department. The BBC
Chairman and Director-General assured the
committee that religious programmes would not
be marginalized and that religious programmes
would continue to have a key role in the BBC's
public service broadcasting commitment.

1993 – The Central Religious Advisory Committee reiterated its criticism of the move of Religious Broadcasting to Manchester. The BBC said the relocation
would not damage its work. *Songs of Praise* was
moved a little earlier to 6.25 p.m.

1994 – Radio 5 Live was launched. Unlike its predecessor,
Radio 5, it carried no religion. Viewing figures rose
for *Heart of the Matter*. Educational series such as
Glimpses of God and *Faith to Faith* preceded Sunday
worship on BBC 1. *Telling Tales* was there for children. The long-running *This is the Day* (BBC 1
Sunday) ended.

1995 – *Songs of Praise* (in its 35th year) broadcast all year at
6.25 p.m. *Heart of the Matter* and *Everyman* together
covered virtually the whole year (48 weeks).
Morning worship lasted for 45 minutes and featured *Heart and Soul*, *A Word in Season*, *The Promise
of His Glory* and *First Light*.

1996 – *Songs of Praise* transmission times fluctuated between 5.55 and 6.20 p.m., although this was still in peak time.

1997 – *Songs of Praise* started throughout the year just after 6 p.m. Sunday morning religious television ran from 9.30 to 10.15 a.m. The main change this year was the marked reduction in the number of editions of *Heart of the Matter* and *Everyman*.

1998 – The Radio 4 schedule changed markedly in April, placing *Sunday* between 7 and 8 a.m. and the morning worship just after 8 a.m. The BBC television Sunday morning worship was abandoned in September and was replaced by *The Heaven and Earth Show*, a magazine programme. *Songs of Praise*, on occasion, started as early as 5.40 p.m. – outside peak time for the first time. There was, for the first time, no formal worship on BBC television on Christmas Day morning.

1999 – Network radio religious output fell by 15 per cent within a single programme year, 1998/99. *The Big End (of the world)* ran for seven weeks in the late Sunday slot in the winter. The Head of Religious Broadcasting described it as 'flawed'. The late evening religious programmes were fewer and those which remained were screened later, often beginning at 11.25 p.m. *Songs of Praise* started earlier, often at 5.30 p.m. The Director of Television announced that from 2000, *Everyman* would begin no later than 10.40 p.m.

2000 – A special *Songs of Praise* for the first Sunday of 2000 drew 66,000 people to the new stadium in Cardiff for a live broadcast on BBC 1. This followed national services on BBC 2 for each of the four nations. BBC 2 produced *Seeing Salvation* to coincide with the exhibition at the National Gallery in London. The

General Synod of the Church of England, the Methodist Conference and the Assembly of the United Reformed Church all considered the nature and content of religious broadcasting. Two days before the General Synod debate it was announced that the weekday repeat of *Songs of Praise*, withdrawn some years earlier, would be reinstated. BBC Scotland once again gave impressive coverage to the General Assembly of the Church of Scotland – 3 hours 10 minutes on BBC 2, two hours of which were in peak time. BBC Radio Scotland devoted four hours to special coverage. BBC Wales postponed plans to cut its religious radio budget by 40 per cent by removing producer posts and abandoning worship programmes following 700 letters of objection and petitions from churches.

Appendix D

Religious Television Programmes on a Sample Sunday – 1999

BBC 1 – *Heaven and Earth Show* – 9.30–10.30 a.m.

There was minimal religious content; the first such reference came 27 minutes into the programme during an extended trail for that evening's *Songs of Praise* from Wigan when a rugby league player spoke briefly of his Christian conversion (3 minutes). Other contents: A discussion on nationalism and patriotism with three studio guests (7 minutes). A disabled woman took 'a sideways look' at Monet and his failing eyesight. (This was more than three minutes straight to camera with references to disabled painters she knew but without shots of their work or that of Monet.) Next were vox pops in Manchester on nationality followed by another three studio guests, two black, on national identity. Religious identity was not raised here or elsewhere.

After the *Songs of Praise* extended trail there were clips from a recent BBC television docu-soap, *Paddington Green*, and a studio interview with a sex-changed prostitute who had been featured (9 minutes). There was no moral dimension to the questioning. Then came an item recorded at a car boot sale about the participants' motivations. People enjoyed the drab surroundings early on a wet Sunday morning. It made church services look cushy by comparison. But the interviewer did not refer to alternative activities which might be considered on such a day. After seven minutes of video it was back to the discussion on national identity for a further four minutes.

The star guest was athlete, Roger Black, in a location interview. Reference was made to his childhood roles as chorister and server but he said: 'I now avoid all that.' We discovered that he was soon to marry in a French church, 'but I don't have to be a Roman Catholic'. The two presenters, Kevin Woodford and Catrina Skepper, were far from impressive and the production values were low. Altogether it was pedestrian and boring. Heaven lost to Earth.

ITV – *Sunday Morning* – 10.30–11.30 a.m.

This is an Anglia production for ITV regions, not Scottish. It opened with a religious dance sequence followed by a six-minute interview with the Methodist minister, Rob Frost, handled by two presenters who were much better than their BBC counterparts. Rob spoke of his pre-Millennium touring shows and was aiming to 'lift eyes above commercialism' and 'taking the Lord's Prayer and interpreting it'. This was followed by a four-minute pilgrimage profile of Malta, one of a series of six such religious features and was visually interesting, if predictable. Then came *Daily Telegraph* agony aunt, Anne Atkins, who takes every opportunity to talk about faith issues in real-life situations. The first 34 minutes rounded off with a built feature at a home for spiritual and Christian healing, which included a teenage girl who had suffered from depression saying 'God has changed me.'

The 15-minute worship element was introduced and linked by the Reverend Leslie Griffiths. This was well handled. Viewer participation allowed for prayer requests to be seen along the foot of the screen in a way that BBC Sunday morning television used to employ.

ITV – *My Favourite Hymns* – 11.30–12 noon

This week John Stapleton spoke to Rosemary Conley about how 'giving her life to the Lord' in 1986 had radically changed her outlook and behaviour. She spoke of reading the Bible and praying, of moving away from the Church of England to an evangelical church and of the happiness that her faith brought, as well as the material success of her diet books. Discipline was required both of the slimmer and the believer. This was a Granada production which lasted for 24 minutes.

BBC 1 – *Songs of Praise* – 5.30–6.05 p.m.

This series maintains a consistent standard demonstrating high production values. Its range of interviewees reflects the impact of faith in people's lives. However, the tendency to move away from traditional church settings has alienated some viewers. The programme has inherited many who previously enjoyed ITV's *Highway* at this time, though the placing has moved ever earlier and is now no longer classified by the BBC as peak time.

BBC 1 – *The Big End* – 11.25–11.55 p.m.

Simon Mayo presented *The Big End (of the world)* from a public house in Camden Town. This was a fast-moving programme, so fast that many of the items lasted less than two minutes. In the main they merited less! Here is a flavour: Instant Karma – Vince Rogers. New Age supporters are being encouraged to sample etherium gold, bottles of which are imported from America and sell for £30. This was described as 'Viagra for the Soul – a supplement for the spirit'. Manchester City supporters were told to 'swallow with reverence' but reported no discernible benefit.

The presenter then appeared to imply that religion was at the root of the world's problems. The first of a series of irritating interludes followed, of people in the street trying to sing hymns, prior to the presenter interviewing an American correspondent, transsexual nun, Sister Paula, the owner of a cable television station. Next came a two-minute cartoon entitled *'Farmer Geddon'* after which a boy artist showed a stone he had found in the shape of a human head. This lasted one minute.

The following minute or two appeared to be a plug for two horoscope books; one called *'Water Magic – wash away your worries'* and the second *'Winning with Witchcraft'*. The presenter handled this light-heartedly but they were given credibility when he read out the addresses from which they could be obtained whilst the camera showed the application forms. After more hymn singing in the street, there was a very brief visit to the D-Day Communications bunker in Sussex which once served as a county nuclear command base.

Three young people in the pub were said to be so nervous about the end of the world that one girl was to have a sex change, the other girl had an embarrassing rash and the boy suffered from flatulence. Presumably this was all inconsequential drivel, a description fitting the next and one of the longest items in the programme. Andy Jones, a printer, once saw a grey pencil-shaped object in the sky. This led to his becoming a born-again Christian, who now spends much of his free time confirming Biblical prophecies from newspaper cuttings and disseminating them. For example, in the British Telecom logo he sees a snake representing the Anti-Christ and Microsoft's logo incorporates three groups of six black squares – no prizes for guessing the implication of this. 'The Lord's given me insight and discernment into what these mean,' said Andy, 'but don't think I'm being paranoid!'

'The Last Judgement' was the title of an interview with the Editor of the *Daily Mirror*, Piers Morgan: 'Boris Yeltsin worries me – too many vodkas – he'll head down to the nuke room, do his crazy dance and he's going to hit it'; 'Bill Clinton performs non-sexual relations with Saddam Hussein's daughter'; 'I see a despot doing something very stupid'; 'I believe in the afterlife. You have to hope to go upstairs rather than down as my mother will write my character reference'; 'I plead guilty to being puerile, a mischief-maker, but not a bad egg.'

A reaction from viewers in the target age group: two intelligent young people in their twenties, who came from a Christian background, not particularly committed, felt that a programme such as this would deter their contemporaries from involvement with religion.

Credits: scriptwriters (2), consultant, production co-ordinator, assistant, manager, executives (2), researchers (3), assistant producers (3), associate producers (2), executive producer, producer, series producer. One called Reith; no relation it is to be hoped!

Appendix E

BBC UK Religious Output and Percentage of Total Output

Year	TV Hours	TV Percentage	Radio Hours	Radio percentage
1936	*			6.24
1950–51	5	0.3	380	3.0
1951–52	9	0.5	410	3.0
1952–53	18	1.0	386	3.0
1953–54	31	1.6	412	3.0
1954–55	26	1.2	406	3.0
1955–56	33	1.3	397	3.0
1956–57	48	1.8	409	3.0
1957–58	57	1.9	404	2.9
1958–59	70	2.2	431	3.0
1959–60	70	2.2	430	3.0
1960–61	83	2.5	426	3.0
1961–62	82	2.4	421	3.0
1962–63	138	4.1	444	3.0
1963–64	141	4.0	455	3.0
1964–65	139	2.5**	461	3.0
1965–66	150	2.6	445	2.0
1966–67	151	2.5	426	2.0
1967–68	152	2.5	479	2.0***
1968–69	151	2.4	381	2.0
1969–70	153	2.3	415	2.0
1970–71	146	2.2	416	1.8
1971–72	143	2.1	451	1.9
1972–73	144	1.8	455	1.8

*   BBC TV opens
**   BBC 2 opens
***   Radio 1 opens

Year	TV Hours	TV Percentage	Radio Hours	Radio percentage
1973–74	162	2.0	431	1.6
1974–75	145	1.7	421	1.6
1975–76	137	1.6	438	1.8
1976–77	139	1.6	447	1.9
1977–78	140	1.6	448	1.8
1978–79	134	1.5	419	1.5
1979–80	145	1.5	458	1.5
1980–81	142	1.5	464	1.6
1981–82	149	1.5	512	1.7
1982–83	149	1.5	436	1.5
1983–84	144	1.3	410	1.4
1984–85	147	1.4	526	1.7
1985–86	166	1.6	417	1.4
1986–87	147	1.3	420	1.4
1987–88	177	1.5	396	1.3
1988–89	173	1.4	428	1.4
1989–90	167	1.3	397	1.3
1990–91	149	1.2	485	1.4*
1991–92	100	0.8	513	1.3
1992–93	107	0.8	470	1.2
1993–94	129	1.0	472	1.2
1994–95	145	1.1	471	1.2**
1995–96	152	1.1	512	1.3
1996–97	122	0.8	553	1.3
1997–98	112	0.7	518	1.2
1998–99	122	0.7	439	1.0
1999–00	117	0.7	435	1.0
* Radio 5 opens				
** R5 Live opens				

Source: BBC Handbooks and Annual Reports

SUFFERERS and OTHERS "LISTENING-IN."

How many are there who "listen-in" who long to hear something daily of God and His love?

We are told of the great numbers of wireless sets installed in hospitals and nursing homes, and we rejoice. But do those who so generously bring these gifts within reach of the pillows of the sick, realise the feelings and thoughts of those who lie there suffering?

Life is a very real affair, and often so terribly grim to a large proportion of them (as well as to many others among the vast audience) that secular music—however sweet and inspiring some of it may be—and variety-turns, talks and suchlike—however desirable and helpful as instruction or pastime, fail altogether to satisfy the desperate need of something deeper, whereon the soul may rest.

Surely the time has come for such need to be met, even though a section of listeners incline to raise objections on the ground that they personally would be bored. And, after all, we know that these are really warm-hearted people who will, for the most part, cheerfully consent to give up half-an-hour a day—say just after the children's hour—when invalids are ready to settle down for the night.

Indeed, since there is such wonderful opportunity of bringing peace and hope to those who are sick or sad, dare we, *dare any of us*, any longer withhold them?

Almost every day there are some amongst those who "listen-in" who listen for the last time before passing on into eternity.

Will all listeners who are in sympathy with this suggestion please sign the appeal? When complete to be posted to

K. M. C.,

THE COTTAGE,

WATFORD.

We greatly appreciate the Sunday evening Wireless Services, and the Evensong relayed weekly from Westminster Abbey; but all the more because these are precious to so many do we plead earnestly for a *daily* consecrated half-hour.

We believe that we shall get this. Already nearly five thousand letters and signatures have been received. Many of them of a most touching nature, from blind, bedridden and aged folk. Bishops, clergy, ministers of all denominations, doctors, sisters and nurses have united to encourage us to press on.

Please send a long list of signatures without delay, remembering that each *one* counts.

[P.T.O. FOR SIGNATURES.

Miss Cordeux's campaign in 1926 ensured BBC daily worship for 70 years